Talk About Understanding

"Ellin takes her masterful guidance to a new level, modeling how educators can teach children to understand more deeply and more lastingly. Her focus on getting all children to understand more deeply and lastingly is unwavering and based on her belief that all learners can, and she provides a clear map of how to help them get there. As a leader of a dual language school, I am especially appreciative of how this book is relevant to those who teach second language learners—by focusing on how to tap into student's schema and provide access to and develop content knowledge, higher-order thinking, and the use of oral language—all essential for second language learners. At a time when we hear much rhetoric about higher standards with little guidance on how to reach them, Ellin provides yet another welcome tool for literacy educators that will help us take literacy teaching to the next level."

—**Julie Nora,** Ph.D., Director
International Charter School

"For many years now, teachers have been helping children develop an awareness of the strategies that critical readers use as they process and make sense of text, yet we are often perplexed about how to improve the quality and depth of student responses. What exactly are we looking for and how do we get there? Ellin provides teachers with a vision to take strategy instruction to the next level by understanding how our language plays a crucial role in building true understanding."

—**Barb Keister**
Literacy Coordinator
Delaware City Schools

Ellin Oliver Keene

Talk About Understanding

Rethinking Classroom Talk to Enhance Comprehension

HEINEMANN
Portsmouth, NH

Heinemann

361 Hanover Street

Portsmouth, NH 03801–3912

www.heinemann.com

Offices and agents throughout the world

The author and publisher wish to thank those who have generously given permission to reprint borrowed material in this book and/or on the DVD:

One Green Apple by Eve Bunting. Text copyright © 2006 by Edward D. Bunting and Anne E. Bunting Family Trust. Illustrations copyright © 2006 by Ted Lewin Ltd. Reprinted by permission of Houghton Mifflin Harcourt Publishing Company. All rights reserved.

(*credits continue on page 160*)

Library of Congress Cataloging-in-Publication Data

Keene, Ellin Oliver.

    Talk about understanding : rethinking classroom talk to enhance comprehension / Ellin Oliver Keene.

       p. cm.

    Includes bibliographical references.

    ISBN-13: 978-0-325-02839-2

    ISBN-10: 0-325-02839-7

    1. Listening comprehension—Study and teaching. 2. Communication in education. 3. Affective education. 4. Discourse analysis. I. Title.

    LB1065.K375 2012

    372.69—dc23   2011043744

Editor: Thomas Newkirk

Production: Sarah Weaver

Production coordination: Patricia Adams

Cover and interior designs: Lisa Fowler

Typesetter: Gina Poirier Design

Manufacturing: Steve Bernier

Video producer: Kevin Carlson

Video editor: Sherry Day

Printed in the United States of America on acid-free paper

20 19 18 ML 3 4 5

For my sister-in-law, Andrea,
Courage personified.
Hers is a voice that speaks clearly
of what it means to understand

deeply and lastingly.

Contents

PART 1   **IDEAS THAT LAST**

From the Inside

VIDEO SEGMENTS

From the Inside chapters (Chapters 3, 5, and 7) focus on one lesson in depth and are accompanied with video. Readers can read all the way through the chapter and go back to watch the accompanying video or can stop at designated places in the chapter and view the video section that corresponds to the lesson's written description. *From the Inside* chapters highlight the use of the **Outcomes of Understanding** and the **Talk About Understanding Principles** in real classroom settings.

PART 2 WORDS THAT MATTER

ON THE WEB — APPENDICES

To see the appendices, go to www.heinemann.com/products/E02839.aspx and click on the Companion Resources tab.

Acknowledgments

It is customary to thank the people who have contributed their intellectual energy, emotional support, or editorial expertise, which of course I will do here. But, as I thought about the support I received as I wrote this book, I have to acknowledge another, very significant factor. It's my house. I love my house. It's not in any way grand or impressive. It's just a simple Cape Cod (complete with a white picket fence) on a quiet city block in Denver. It is serene and, to me, beautiful. It pleases my sense of the aesthetic (see Chapter 2) and I love to tinker around in it. No one else would consider it remarkable, but when I return from almost-weekly travels, it wraps me up in its arms, sharing its familiar smells, funny, tucked-away cupboards and closets, and creaking floorboards, its office full of books and the yard flanked by huge hackberry and birch trees. I can think here. I can write here.

Today, I'm writing in the family room, looking out to the late summer sun through the leaves of the hackberry and across the patio to the huge purple and orange salvia I planted in May. In the winter, I write in the living room or bedroom in front of the fire with a shawl around my shoulders and fuzzy socks on my feet. One or more of the three basset hounds (Chaucer, Toby, and Lucy) that call this place home sprawl on the floor. The late afternoon light is filtered through the birch on that side of the house and in autumn the leaves make the interior spaces glow. I can write here. I can think here.

I need to have the laundry running, the counters clean, the rooms tidied, the dogs fed, the emails answered, and the travel plans made before I can sit down to focus on writing. Hence, my now infamous delays in submitting chapters! I would like to say here that it's my house's fault. It gives me the gift of all these mundane chores, helps me procrastinate; it gives me something small to think about, something I can do that will make an immediate, visible difference. So, thank you, house. Thank you for your sweetness and your sanctuary, for giving me work to do and a place to think and write.

I am fortunate to publish with the incomparable Heinemann, which provides me with another home in which I can experiment with ideas and write about what is urgently on my mind. Kate Montgomery, publisher, has provided gentle guidance, razor-sharp insights, and abundant patience at every juncture. I would follow her to the ends of the earth! Sarah Fournier, Patty Adams, and Elizabeth Valway were so available and helpful in the post-writing stages. I begged for Sarah Weaver, who edited *To Understand*, to come back for this project and her contributions, again, went way beyond edits—she made the content stronger. She is a very gifted editor and I'm more than appreciative.

I have also had the extraordinary opportunity to work in the landscape of professional development for Heinemann and to be part of their family of thinkers. Vicki Boyd, dear friend and constant inspiration, has invited me to be part of crafting professional learning for educators through a wonderful professional learning community of Heinemann consultants, the residencies in which I get to work with schools and districts for extended periods of time and as editor of the Heinemann Professional Development catalogue/journal. This work challenges me and diversifies my work and I'm very grateful to be along for the ride with Vicki, Michelle Flynn, Cherie Bartlett, Jonathan Higgins, Donna Robillard, Pat Goodman, and the rest of the professional learning gang there.

Vicki and I work with an extraordinary group of Heinemann consultants in a professional learning community. Through our annual retreats and monthly phone calls, Colleen Buddy, Jennifer Phillips, Jen McDonough, Jill DeGoede, Kathy Collins, Ian Fleischer, Louise Wrobleski, Tomasen Carey, Karen Caine, Tiffany Boyd, Matt Glover, and Mary Alice Berry provided invaluable direction on an early draft of *Talk About Understanding*, but the greatest gift is their willingness to engage in ongoing conversation with me about the things that matter most in our work. Their knowledge and their unswerving values about bringing our best to children inspire me.

This book and video have a setting, and it is Midlothian, Illinois—specifically, Kolmar Elementary, where I have been privileged to work for three years. Carrie Cahill, assistant superintendent, is one of those rare people who lead skillfully from a deep knowledge base about literacy. She and our colleague and friend Kathy Horvath made my frequent visits to the Chicago area stimulating and so much fun it should be illegal—maybe it was! Carrie made it possible for us to film in Midlothian and Cathy Thompson, principal extraordinaire at Kolmar, was grace under pressure when the camera equipment rolled into her school. I learn so much from Carrie, Kathy H., and Cathy T. and am very indebted. Special thanks go to Erin Johnson, Kelly Young, and Dana Murphy, who opened their classrooms to me and the film crew. They do the skillful, compassionate, thoughtful work with those great kids every day. Lucky, lucky kids.

My heartfelt thanks go to Kevin Carlson and his crew, who filmed the video for *Talk About Understanding*. He brought a semitruck's worth of equipment into the classrooms and somehow made the children and teachers feel like it was just another day. Kevin was unendingly patient with me when I was camera-shy and cotton-mouthed. In the end, we laughed more than we cried, and he captured the children whose gorgeous faces and brilliant thinking populate the video sections of this project. Kevin edited it expertly, then handed it over to Sherry Day for the finishing touches back at Heinemann. This was my first foray into the video world and Kevin and Sherry cushioned the blow!

I have also been privileged to work for seven years (as part of a Heinemann residency) in Blue Springs School District outside of Kansas City. I couldn't have imagined, when I began that work, how important the Blue Springs administrators, teachers, and students would become to me. To say that I have learned from this extensive work is an understatement. I have watched the evolution from a district where good things were happening to one in which the vast majority of schools and classrooms are ones to which I would take any colleague in the country (as I've already done!) to observe highly effective instruction. I especially thank my dear friend Jennifer Phillips, instructional coach, Annette Seago, assistant superintendent, and their colleagues Jennie Alderman, Kelly Flax, Amanda Carey, and Pat Dade, and all of the superb literacy coaches. The adventure I have shared with them has been among the most meaningful in my professional life.

I would also like to thank my long-term clients Jerry O'Shea, Katie Minkalis, and their colleagues in Marquardt District 15 outside of Chicago and, again, Kathy Horvath and her colleagues in Northbrook, Illinois. Every trip was a learning experience and a great time. Hard to beat.

I'll never understand why, but every time I ask Tom Newkirk, a professor at the University of New Hampshire, to work with me on a new project, he agrees. Lucky me. Tom's infallible sense of the big picture for the project saved me from myself on at least two significant revisions and he provided innumerable and invaluable suggestions throughout the writing and taping. Neither of us had experience in weaving a book and video project together, but we muddled through. Actually there's no one I'd rather muddle through with because Tom makes me laugh—big, hearty, snorting, loud laughter that we have shared for over fifteen years. We find ourselves hilarious when no one else would crack a smile.

I cannot overstate the role my friends play in my life. Though I don't usually torture them by asking them to read drafts of my writing, they are very much a part of my work. They are the extended family upon whom I rely heavily. In particular, Bruce, Laura, Carol, Mary, and Barb are unending sources of joy, intellectual stimulation, and support. When I close the computer, it's so often to them I gravitate and I'm deeply grateful for their unconditional love. I return it.

Finally, I acknowledge the people to whom I will always owe the greatest thanks—my own little family. David, Elizabeth, and Edward, my nephew, are my anchors and my greatest joy.

PRELUDE

Ideas That Last,
Words That Matter

I've occupied my mind for well over a decade with the question, What does it mean to understand deeply? I mention this so that anyone who, in my youth, accused me of having a short attention span—this means you, Dad, and you, Miss Schakelford—can be dissuaded of their erroneous beliefs! I can't seem to stop thinking about what it means to understand deeply and what conditions enhance that experience for learners all along the age spectrum. The question inevitably leads to other questions: How do we know if we understand deeply? What indicators can we look for to see if children understand deeply, especially when their oral and written language hasn't developed to the point where we can use it to evaluate understanding? How can we rethink instruction to encourage deeper understanding?

I try to read everything I can get my hands on related to these questions, and many writers, colleagues, and friends have contributed enormously to my thinking. In the end, though, I find I like to explore the questions in my own ways, in my own time. I want to provide not answers but hypotheses for readers to test, revise, and reinvent. It's the process of creating a way to understand understanding that holds my attention, and it's that same process I hope other readers will engage in as they read this book and view the video footage.

What does it mean to understand deeply? The poet Percy Bysshe Shelley, nearly two centuries ago, wrote, "A man, to be greatly good, must imagine intensely and comprehensively; he must put himself in the place of another and of many others; the pains and pleasures of his species must become his own." Shelley writes here of empathy and links it to living a good life. Can empathy be taught? Should it be taught? I'm not certain of the answers, but can you imagine our world if empathy was an objective toward which all people strived? Empathy is more than compassion; it involves effort. It demands conscious deliberation focused on the thoughts and emotions of another. It is a powerful brew of thought and feeling. In my view, empathy is a highly evolved juxtaposition of human emotion and cognition and is often present when we understand deeply.

I wonder, too, about the idea of aesthetic sensibility. Is it part of deep understanding? I've come to believe that responding to ideas and art must also be an advanced state of understanding, of experiencing the world around us—a way of being "greatly good." If I take Shelley's statement as a question and ask, "In what ways are we humans greatly good?" several other qualities come to mind. For example, does a person edge closer to "greatly good" if she advocates for other people and takes action on their behalf? Is the propensity to pause and reflect on an idea important to the development of our species? What about nurturing a great and passionate curiosity? Is it important to evaluate one's most deeply held values and beliefs in order to understand the impact they may have on our actions?

Are those qualities associated with living a good life? And surely living a good life includes understanding deeply. Might that mean those qualities are associated with true understanding?

I've been considering these ideas for some time and, of course, my ruminations often turn to children and our responsibilities as parents and teachers. Does it fall into our purview as teachers to help children develop qualities such as empathy, curiosity, and advocacy? In what context do we address such issues? What is our role in classrooms? In what ways do we work toward ever-deeper understanding alongside our students? These are the questions I'd like to explore in *Talk About Understanding*, but it's best to start with our feet firmly planted on the ground, thinking about one great kid, in one classroom on a very typical day in a very typical school.

Marco is a fourth grader on a mission. He has the book *A Fine, Fine School* by Sharon Creech under his arm; he has his reader's notebook and a sharpened pencil in his hand, and he's off to his regular spot to read on this early winter morning. His teacher, Mary Louise, works to direct some of Marco's less-focused colleagues to their reading spots as he settles in, carefully places his bookmark under his leg, and dives into the book. A visitor to the classroom, I watch him from across the room and am impressed with Marco's direction and focus. I mention this to Mary Louise.

"He's a great kid and really into Sharon Creech's books right now, but I'd like for you to confer with him today. I'm not sure what to say to him—where to go with him." She explained that Marco's entries in his reader's notebook somehow lacked the passion she knew he had for Sharon Creech books and for reading in general. She began to question whether she was asking too much of the students with respect to their responses in the notebooks. She told me that she wants responding in reader's notebooks to be an authentic experience for children and uses them because she has to have a way to check in on the students' reading when she can't confer with everyone every day. But, she's worried about the depth of thought—or lack thereof—in the notebooks. "I just haven't seen the progress in thinking in their notebooks, and particularly with Marco. His entries are just very flat." Mary Louise paused for a moment. "You know, given that it's December, I'm getting concerned. My kids just don't seem to understand deeply."

Mary Louise went on to tell me that her comprehension instruction focuses on thinking aloud about comprehension strategies as she reads rich, interesting literature and informational texts. She has worked all year to make certain that the children are choosing books that are appropriately challenging and have engaging material. She has encouraged the children to read in a wide range of genres, but she is increasingly concerned that the children don't seem to be really digging into these great books.

"The books I use in lessons and many of the books they're reading are very thought-provoking, but the kids seem to be missing the heart of these books," Mary Louise told me. "Sometimes, all I get is a few words in discussions and conferences or in their reader's notebooks about a connection they've made or a question they have. As I'm describing this, I realize that I don't just need help with Marco, I need to know how to help all of my kids understand more deeply."

As I listened to Mary Louise, I began to wonder if the lack of depth she was seeing in the children's written responses to text had something to do with her oral language in the classroom—specifically her think-alouds—the talk with children about how she goes about understanding. Thinking aloud is challenging, to say the least. In the past ten to fifteen years, many of us have worked hard to perfect the process of thinking aloud in the classroom. We select books we intend to read aloud, carefully plotting where we might stop to think aloud in order to clarify the meaning and show children how a proficient reader comes to understand. But, how often do we pause to think aloud? How long should a think-aloud be? How quickly do we involve children in sharing their thinking? Should our think-alouds be related to the content of the text, the comprehension strategy we're studying, or both?

I have noticed that think-alouds, which are the heart of comprehension instruction, don't always lead students to think more deeply, so I set about studying my own (through video) and other teachers' think-alouds, searching for examples of talk that led to deeper thinking as well as patterns that appeared to shut thinking down. I quickly realized that Mary Louise's question went well beyond thinking aloud. Our oral language throughout the day has a profound impact on what students retain and reapply. The key question is, how we can modify our teaching to help children understand more deeply and lastingly?

Following the publication of Peter Johnston's important book, *Choice Words* (2004), many of us have become more aware of the ways we talk to kids, but I sense that it's time to focus more directly on how our oral language directly affects the depth of their understanding. There is a real difference between superficial and deep understanding, and our talk in the classroom is the tool we use to bridge that gap. I hear from teachers who know that their students are equipped (with the tools proficient readers often use—comprehension strategies) to deepen their comprehension and make books and ideas more memorable, more useful. However, many, like Mary Louise, have a sense that students could go further—they know their students are capable of much deeper thinking, much more of the time. Comprehension strategies are useful, but teachers are asking, what's next and how do I modify my teaching to get there?

In *Mosaic of Thought* (1997, 2007), my coauthor Susan Zimmermann and I explored a variety of topics related to comprehension strategy instruction and argued that by teaching strategies, we can affect the quality and depth of what students understand and remember. In *Assessing Comprehension Thinking Strategies* (Keene 2006), I provided questions and rubrics to help track students' progress in using comprehension strategies. In *To Understand* (2008), I went further to suggest that comprehension strategies and a focus on what matters most in the literacy curriculum can actually lead to more intellectual engagement and higher levels of thinking for all children, regardless of their present performance level in reading. I sought to bring thousands of children into discussions related to quality literature and informational text and to ensure that we teachers expect the highest levels of thinking from all kids, all the time. In *Comprehension Going Forward* (2011), my colleagues and I argued for a more thoughtful

There is a real difference between superficial and deep understanding, and our talk in the classroom is the tool we use to bridge that gap.

approach to strategy instruction and called for renewed focus on helping students build rich and varied background knowledge through a wide range of texts.

In this book I want to examine the all-important link between our verbal and nonverbal messages in the classroom and the depth and staying power of children's comprehension. In particular, I explore this question: How can we modify our oral communication with children to help them understand more deeply? To do that, I investigate each part of that question—first, what *is* deeper understanding, and second, how do we rethink our language to help them achieve it? We may agree or disagree on the question of whether understanding deeply is part of what it takes to live a life that is "greatly good," but I imagine that everyone who works with children longs for them to understand deeply and lastingly.

*H*ow can we modify the ways we communicate with children to help them understand more deeply?

Part 1: Ideas That Last

What helps a child retain and reapply information she has learned or concepts about which she has read? Why do children seem to forget a concept we were sure they understood when we initially taught it? Why do particular learning experiences seem more meaningful and memorable to children? What does it mean to understand more deeply? Can teachers affect the depth with which our students understand?

To examine these questions I begin, in Chapter 1, to explore our experience in teaching comprehension strategies and argue that strategies are critical tools for children working to comprehend more effectively. But there are new vistas to explore in strategy instruction; we can move beyond superficial use of strategies to help children reach greater depth in their comprehension and ensure that concepts they learn have better staying power. In Chapters 2 and 4, I explore a new model called the Outcomes of Understanding. The outcomes are a set of descriptors we can use to reflect on what deeper understanding is. We'll explore the outcomes as markers that may indicate when children understand deeply and examine how we can modify the ways we interact with students to promote that depth in narrative and informational text. In Chapters 3 and 5, we'll take a look (through text and video) at two in-depth lessons in which I work to push comprehension strategy instruction forward and to demonstrate some of the outcomes in narrative and then in informational texts.

Part 2: Words That Matter

In Chapter 6, I take a look at common, almost habitual patterns we tend to use in our oral interactions with children and argue that these patterns may impede deeper understanding as it was described in Part 1. I propose a new set of guidelines, the Talk About Understanding Principles, that I hope will help us to break out of some ineffective oral language patterns and make modifications in the ways we initiate oral language interactions with children—especially during instruction. We'll look at five of these ten principles at work in group settings and in one-on-one conferences. Chapter 7 provides another in-depth look at a single lesson (through text and video) in which I try to integrate the Outcomes of Understanding and the Talk About Understanding Principles. In Chapter 8, we explore the second five Talk About Understanding Principles. The postlude is a short reflection on the reasons I think it is worthwhile to help children understand more deeply.

On the Web

Be sure to visit the book's website, www.heinemann.com/products/E02839.aspx (click on the Companion Resources tab), for all the appendices. Some provide detailed summaries of the comprehension strategies and the workshop activities presented in the book. Appendix A ("Literacy Studio Components"), for example, outlines the four reader's workshop components I wrote about in *To Understand*. Other appendices provide tools you can download and use in your classroom, such as the "Oral Language Reflection Tool" and the "Observation Record."

How to Use the DVD That Accompanies
Talk About Understanding

The chapters that have accompanying DVD footage (Chapters 3, 5, and 7) are designed to be experienced in several different ways. You have the choice to read the chapter entirely (each stands alone, just like any other chapter) or to pause as you read and view segments of accompanying video. You might also want to watch the video in its entirety before going back to read the chapter. Another option is to view each one of the video segments in a study group, followed by quickly reading the paragraphs that accompany it and discussing both.

My goal in this book and the accompanying video is to show how children understand more deeply when they are treated to more sophisticated and aesthetically pleasing language and how they often adopt those newer language patterns into their daily interactions with adults and other children. To that end, I dig in deeply to explore the many nuances in three particular lessons rather than take a fleeting look at many lessons. There are certainly moments when, upon viewing the video, I wondered if I wouldn't be more gainfully employed selling towels at Macy's! Watching oneself teach on video is a humbling experience, but I want the viewer/reader to see lessons, warts and all, on which they might build. These video segments are not meant, in any way, to be perfect lessons—merely a starting place for professional conversation.

Whether you read and view the videos alone or alongside colleagues, my hope is that they will lead to more powerful classroom interactions and ultimately, deeper, more permanent understanding for children.

*W*atching oneself teach on video is a humbling experience, but I want the viewer/reader to see lessons, warts and all, on which they might build.

Talk About Understanding

PART 1: **IDEAS THAT LAST**

Chapters 1–5 explore what it means to understand

deeply in narrative and informational text and introduce

the *Outcomes of Understanding*, a set of markers

often present when children move beyond rote use of

comprehension strategies to understanding more

deeply and lastingly.

CHAPTER

Comprehension Strategy Instruction Grows Up

Why strategies matter and when they are not enough

"I don't know why we have to make text-to-text, text-to-world, and text-to-self connections again. I did that in elementary and last year." Shanaya, a seventh grader, addresses the class impatiently. Jen, their teacher, explains that Shanaya and the other seventh graders are working in more difficult text and in new genres, which makes it almost like learning a new strategy each year. The strategy is the same, but the texts they read are definitely getting tougher, and it's important to use the strategy in new ways. Shanaya seems to consider this and is just about to speak her rebuttal, but Jen moves on to think aloud about her connections. She's worried, though. Like Mary Louise (introduced in the prelude), she has a nagging feeling that the kids could be thinking at a higher level and that their written and oral responses to strategy instruction are superficial.

Later that day, Jen and her colleagues huddled around a teachers' lounge table still somewhat sticky from the lunch rush hours before. I sat nearby facilitating the conversation. They combed through students' work and shared their own set of frustrations. Jen told the group about Shanaya's query and revealed that today's episode was far from the first time she has heard a similar grievance.

"I know that kids need strategy instruction each year in progressively more difficult text and in new genres, but I can't help but think that I'm missing something," she tells her colleagues. "It's not just that my kids are complaining about learning the same strategies; I think the kids could be going further. Some of their responses are superficial. It's almost like they've figured out the strategy game. 'I made a text-to-text connection . . .'" Her voice trails off. "Part of me wants to say, 'So what'?"

The other teachers laughed, but expressed similar concerns. Carol, one of Jen's colleagues, spoke up. "I know what you mean, and I had just started to believe that my comprehension instruction was working pretty well. I understand the comprehension strategies, I pay attention to how I use them myself, I think aloud using the strategies so my thinking is transparent to kids, I follow up in conferences to ensure that they are applying the strategies, and I try to keep track of their progress using rubrics. But— and I can't quite put my finger on this—I feel like there's more they could be doing. I don't want this to become rote. When I first started teaching comprehension strategies, they'd never had that kind of instruction before and we were all excited. Now the elementary teachers are working on strategies and I feel like it's up to us to dig deeper."

"That may be true, but I have a friend who teaches elementary and she says that kids and teachers are saying the same thing there," Laura added.

Finally, Barb, a seventh-grade teacher, said, "Let's record this because I think we're saying the same thing and I really feel the need to figure it out.

We know the kids can understand more deeply, but we need to know how to get them there and we need some way to know when and if they do comprehend more deeply. Is that right?"

She wrote on chart paper:

1. How can we help children understand more deeply?

2. How do we know when they comprehend deeply?

"I want to clarify where we're going with this," said Grace, an eighth-grade teacher. "I wouldn't want to stop teaching comprehension strategies. Our scores have gone up, the kids are reading more, and they're reading with better comprehension. I think there has even been a spillover to their writing, and now the other people on our team are trying to talk to them about how the strategies work in science, social studies, and math."

Others agreed. Comprehension strategy instruction had made a huge difference in their teaching and in students' learning. They reflected on the improvements in students' work over the last several years and commented that there was lots of good news to hold on to. Students seemed more independent in their reading, specifically in solving comprehension problems. They were more engaged in reading content-area material—they seemed to feel less overwhelmed by it, more able to tackle it with confidence and more able to extract important points. They were also more open to discussion about ideas in books, and they had developed a language (comprehension strategies) to talk to each other about books. There was just a nagging feeling that something was missing.

A Larger View

The good news Jen's study group described coincides with what I've observed in American classrooms. The focus on strategy instruction has been a boost to comprehension in literature and across the content areas and has caused us to reexamine both our teaching and children's learning in a profound way. (See Figure 1.1 for a list of comprehension strategies and see Appendix B, "Comprehension Strategies Defined," on the book's website for a more detailed compendium of key teaching points.) I want to pause for a moment to consider some of the changes I've seen in classrooms since we first read about and began teaching these strategies in the 1980s.

Comprehension strategy instruction:

1. *Caused us to become more reflective about our own reading.* Many of us first discovered the power of comprehension strategies by becoming aware of them in our own reading. We teachers typically hadn't been asked to use strategies in our own schooling and when we became conscious of them, we saw immediately how beneficial strategy instruction would be for children. It wasn't long before we were able to extrapolate from our own reading processes to understand how to think aloud for children, making the complex comprehension processes more transparent.

2. *Created a common language between teachers and kids.* At one time it was too easy to conclude that children didn't understand a text or weren't developmentally "ready" to consider abstract ideas, when in fact what was missing was a common language they could use to describe and define their thinking. When teachers and children share the language of comprehension strategies, what a teacher thinks aloud about today, children can use independently tomorrow and well into the future. Children use the language of strategies to discuss insights and ideas about text and content knowledge in far more depth and across a broader age spectrum than we would have imagined. When children have comprehension strategies in their language arsenal, they are far more likely to retain and reapply what they've read. Asking questions, for example, may cause them to continue to ponder as they read further in a text and is a tool they can use in virtually any text they read at any time. Strategy language gives children and teachers a common reference point to use in discussion about text and content-area concepts, making it much more likely that they'll use the tool in another context.

3. *Led to increased time spent teaching comprehension.* In many classrooms teachers now spend far more time teaching comprehension as opposed to "testing" comprehension by asking children to retell and answer comprehension questions about text. Comprehension strategies have become a means to focus explicit instruction on strategies proficient readers are known to use (Pearson and Gallagher 1983; Pressley 2001). We now know what to teach in comprehension

rather than endlessly assessing comprehension by asking questions and asking students to summarize. When teachers think aloud, the mysterious process of understanding becomes visible and audible for children, permitting them to use the same processes when reading independently. Children awaken the "voice in their minds" and listen as it takes them into the depths of books where they might not have ventured without the strategies.

4. *Generated innovation in classrooms.* Teachers have imagined myriad ways to approach comprehension strategy instruction, from songs related to the strategies to book club discussions to colorful charts designed to serve as a visible reminder of the strategies. They have worked tirelessly to develop approaches to thinking aloud and gradually releasing responsibility to students until they can use the strategies independently. In an era when teachers are increasingly asked to use formulaic prescriptions and scripts in their teaching, strategy instruction has reawakened the artistry in our teaching.

5. *Helped teachers raise expectations for all children.* Teaching comprehension strategies has helped us see how much is possible for all learners when they're taught to think. Time and again, I'm told of children who typically don't share in a large group, are identified for special education, or are less inclined to think deeply but who, when armed with strategies, have the confidence and the language to express their ideas in a way that challenges everyone's thinking about a book. Ours is a nation that gives a great deal of lip service to "higher expectations," but strategy instruction goes beyond the rhetoric to give form and substance to the goal of teaching children to think at high levels. They rise to the occasion time after time.

6. *Made it acceptable to read slowly with depth and focus.* One of the key benefits of using comprehension strategies is that they actually slow kids down—and that's a good thing! In light of schools' measurement of children's reading based on words per minute (not to mention the time children spend with video games, whose images change every second), it's worth remembering that the best thinking often takes the longest time. We need to teach kids to literally slow down and consider ideas they encounter in reading, and

strategies are the tools we use to do so. If I ask a child to consider his inferences, it's going to take a bit of time. Using strategy instruction, we ask kids to pause and ponder, to focus on deeper understanding of texts and concepts, and that is a skill that will last long after we've said goodbye at the end of the year.

7. *Focused our instruction on the reader, not just the text.* In teaching comprehension strategies, we focus on how readers can actually get better at reading rather than on how they answer questions and retell. Most comprehension instruction before strategies focused on asking children to recall details from the text. Now we focus instruction on the mental moves proficient readers make to better understand the ideas and concepts in the text. While it's still critically important to focus on the text/conceptual content, we know now that teaching children to approach and learn content strategically makes it more likely that they'll retain and reapply the concepts about which they read. And in the end, aren't we most concerned with having children remember and reuse what they understand—long after we're there to remind them?

8. *Helped children to build a vast bank of content-area knowledge.* Because children are more likely to retain and reapply what they learn when they are metacognitive (aware of their own thinking and able to manipulate it), we are also teaching them to "hold on" to content knowledge. If, for example, a child learns about whales and is asked to connect that new learning with what she already knows about mammals, it's far more likely that she'll remember the new content about whales. If a child is asked to synthesize following a reading about the Civil War, he is forced to make decisions about what was most important from several sources and texts and to interject his opinions and commentary about the content. Personalizing information makes it stick, and being aware of our own processes in understanding makes ideas last.

Comprehension strategy instruction has yielded a great deal of information with respect to how children use the language of thought. We know that strategies are tools that lead to deeper understanding, but we haven't yet resolved Jen's initial question. Isn't there more? Couldn't kids go deeper into their understanding of text more consistently? If we name the strategies and discuss them with children, why aren't we naming and discussing deeper comprehension? Do we know what deeper comprehension is?

A Plan Emerges

Back in the teachers' lounge, Anna underscored her sense that comprehension strategy instruction had been invaluable. "I agree. I just think that they could go deeper, more often," another added. "I guess this is all good news when you think about it. Our kids are doing more than we could have imagined even five years ago. We're just more ambitious for them. We know now that they're able to do more, and we want them to!"

Henry, a sixth-grade teacher, interjected, "I think the questions we've recorded would be a great focus of a year-long study group. We could read *To Understand* (Keene 2008) together and get a better sense of what it really means to understand more deeply. And, we could experiment with kids; bring their work in to analyze . . . As a matter of fact, I think we should start by talking to the kids about this—we should see what they think. We can ask them to tell us what it means to understand more deeply. I'd be fascinated to hear what my kids would say if asked what it means to understand more deeply—to go beyond the strategies."

"Let's see what they say"

The next day, Jen was eager to put Henry's suggestion to work. What would students say if they were asked what it means to comprehend more deeply? She was also curious to see if it was even possible to cause students to think more deeply about text by changing the way we react to their ideas. How would she know if they were thinking more deeply?

She gathered her students around her in the front of the classroom and spoke honestly to them. "I understand your frustration when you're asked to do something that you believe you've already done. I understand that you've had lots of opportunities when you were younger to learn about the comprehension strategies that help you understand better. Now I think you're ready for the next step." She paused a long moment.

"As your teacher, I want so much for you. I want you to understand some texts so deeply and well that you'll never forget them. I think you're

Comprehension Strategies

Monitoring for Meaning

- Knowing when, as a reader, you fully understand
- Knowing when, as a reader, you don't understand
- Knowing what you need to understand
- Knowing a wide range of fix-up strategies to repair comprehension

Use Schema (Prior Knowledge)

- Relate the new to the known—activate prior knowledge to help understand new information
- Make connections between texts, portions of the same text, the text and broader knowledge, and the text and the reader
- Create schema using in a variety of ways if, as a reader, you realize that you lack the necessary schema to understand a text or concept

Infer

- Predict
- Make independent decisions about inexplicit meanings
- Create meaning to fill in gaps in the text
- Develop interpretations
- Form opinions and defend them
- Draw conclusions and defend them

Ask Questions

- Generate questions before, during and after reading
- Use questions to focus on one aspect of the text, delve more deeply into its meaning, and extrapolate to insights within and beyond the text

Create Images

- Use images that emanate from all five senses to understand more vividly, more deeply
- Use images that emanate from the emotions to understand more vividly, more deeply

Determine Importance

- Decide which ideas and/or concepts are most important in a text
- Articulate why those ideas are most important and what influenced you, as a reader, to focus on them
- Identify key themes and series of events in text
- Extrapolate to less explicit meaning or larger ideas within and beyond the text

Synthesize Information

- Be aware of the evolution of thought during reading—how your thinking changes as you read
- Create a cogent expression of key points after reading—this expression may contain information from a variety of sources outside the current text

Figure 1.1

ready to discover things in text that even the author may not have known were there; I think you're ready to talk about what you read in thoughtful and insightful ways with others; I think you can remember far more from your reading than you do right now and I believe you're ready to let books *affect* you in a profound way. I believe you're ready to come into the world of people who read because the characters and conflicts, the events and themes, the information and ideas actually change them. I think you're ready to read with a different outlook—not only trying to make a connection, but also exploring how your connections really help you understand more effectively. I want this to be a watershed day—a day when we as a class and you individually begin to change the reader you are into the reader you're able to become."

Jen had, perhaps without knowing it, defined deeper understanding in her lesson introduction by describing what she hoped for the children with respect to their experiences with books.

Jen paused a moment. The students stared back. "Uh-oh," she thought, but persevered.

"We have to figure out what helps us understand more deeply. We know comprehension strategies are tools to help readers understand—but what does it mean to understand deeply and well? What does it mean to understand so well that you actually remember ideas for a long time? We have to sort out those questions together, and I think we can use a portion of a book to help us.

"I'm going to read a short piece from Sandra Cisneros' book *The House on Mango Street*. Some of you are reading that book now. The piece I'm going to read aloud to you is an excerpt from it. You all have your reader's notebooks with you; I want you to begin to think about and take some notes on how you work to understand a text. Then I'm going to ask you to read this piece to yourselves and take more notes on how you work to comprehend. Here's what I mean by that. Think about what happens in your minds—what are you thinking that helps you understand? Do you create mental images, do you feel as if you're part of the book in some way, do you wonder things about the book? And, what happens in your lives? What do you do to help yourself understand? Do you reread, do you underline portions of the text, do you make notes, do you understand more by talking to other readers about the text, do you feel like you want to write or draw to fully understand? What do you do in your life in order to understand? Okay? What do you do in your mind and in your life in order to understand? First I'll read aloud, then you'll read and take notes as you're reading, then we'll share."

Beautiful and Cruel

I am an ugly daughter. I am the one nobody comes for.

    Nenny says she won't wait her whole life for a husband to come and get her, that Minerva's sister left her mother's house by having a baby, but she doesn't want to go that way either. She wants things all her own, to pick and choose. Nenny has pretty eyes and it's easy to talk that way if you are pretty.

    My mother says when I get older my dusty hair will settle and my blouse will learn to stay clean, but I have decided not to grow up tame like the others who lay their necks on the threshold waiting for the ball and chain.

    In the movies there is always one with red, red lips who is beautiful and cruel. She is the one who drives the men crazy and laughs them all away. Her power is her own. She will not give it away.

    I have begun my own quiet war. Simple. Sure. I am one who leaves the table like a man, without putting back the chair or picking up the plate.

—FROM SANDRA CISNEROS, THE HOUSE ON MANGO STREET

Jen was asking the students to be aware of the thinking and behaviors that lead to understanding in the first place and, perhaps, to deeper understanding. She read aloud, slowly and expressively, and then asked the students to read the text silently. She reminded them of the ideas she wanted to capture in their reader's notebooks—How did they go about understanding? What happened in their minds and their lives as they read? She was stunned to see them reading and writing furiously. They went back and forth between reading the short piece and writing about their understanding in their reader's notebooks. Jen asked them to share their thinking with a partner but cautioned them, "Remember that you and your partner can talk about the text itself, but I'm most interested in having you talk about how you comprehend. What were you thinking—what I call 'in your mind'—as you read? Did you experience any emotion; did you gain any new perspective? Did you use strategies as tools to help you comprehend? How did that work? And I'd also like for you to discuss what did you actually do—what I call 'in your life'—while you read? Did you reread, did you take notes?"

The pairs talked animatedly for several minutes before Jen brought them back as a large group, gathered around two easels with chart paper, one labeled "In My Mind" and the other, "In My Life." She asked for volunteers to share not what they shared in their conversation, but what their partner said that surprised, excited, or inspired them. There was a moment of confusion in which those students who had raised their hands to share their ideas even before Jen had finished her invitation quickly lowered them and whispered to their partners, "Quick. What did you say, tell me again . . . " Jen's strategy for getting students to listen in a more thoughtful, fully attentive way was working. Finally Jasmine raised her hand.

"My partner was Tiffany and she said that she had connections to her sister." Jen knew that this was one of the classic moments when there really must be more depth to the student's thinking; that the use of the strategy (in this case schematic connections) was the beginning of understanding, but not the outcome. She asked, "I understand that Tiffany had a connection to her sister when she read this. Tiffany, can you tell me how that connection helped you understand this piece better?"

Tiffany paused for a long moment. "I just think that my sister thinks she's the pretty one and she acts like it, but it's really just because she's older."

At one point in her teaching career, Jen would have thanked Tiffany and moved on to another student with his hand raised, but she decided to persist. "Oh, your sister thinks she's the pretty one and acts like that's true." Wisely, Jen reiterated Tiffany's point so that she could hear her own thoughts aloud and have more time to think. Jen continued, "How did thinking about her help you understand this piece better?" This was the turning point—and a very important question if we're interested in deeper understanding.

Tiffany must have known then that she was going to have to respond differently. Jen wasn't asking about the connection anymore, she was acknowledging Tiffany's thinking, but pushing beyond it. Schematic connections do support deeper understanding, but what was it that she understood more completely now that she had made the connection?

"*T*iffany, can you tell me how that connection helped you understand this piece better?"

"Well," Tiffany said after a slightly uncomfortable pause, "I guess it was that I agree that being pretty or hot or something is really overrated. I think that people who might not be that good-looking have the most to say sometimes. I think it gets better because my dad told me that he was never that handsome and it wasn't until he was in college that he felt that people took what he had to say seriously and really listened to him and stuff . . . "

"What else, Tiffany?" Jen interjected.

"I don't know, I just—" Tiffany paused for another moment. "I just think that the girl in here [she indicated the piece] has some real strength because she's not giving in to what other people might do. She's a character that I'd actually like to know. I'm like, I'm really behind what she's doing. When it says that she's starting her war, she's standing up to what people expect from her, and I have always thought and now I think even more that you have to expect a lot from yourself because other people, even your family, may not know what makes you strong. And if you're not pretty, sometimes like that girl, you've got to have real power in you, like inside yourself to surprise people who don't expect that much from you. It's like she's learning that it's good to be smart and that's where her power comes from."

"So, Tiffany, it's really interesting to me because all of your thoughts started out as a connection to your sister, but when I asked you how your connections helped you understand the piece more, you had a lot more to say." Jen used the opportunity to point out that students often think that what they have already said is all they have to say, when there really is much more depth lurking just below the surface. Jen got at that depth by restating what Tiffany had said, asking how the connection helped her understand the piece better, and then simply asking, "What else?" That simple question may be one of the most powerful queries in our repertoire if we want children to think more deeply.

At this point, other students had hands up and were clearly ready to jump into the conversation, but Jen held them off for another moment.

"I want to capture your thinking on one of these easels, Tiffany. Do you think that what you just described belongs on the 'In Your Mind' chart paper or the 'In Your Life' sheet?"

"I would say both," replied Tiffany, "because it was all just stuff I was thinking about, but some of it just came to me when I was talking to Jasmine and you. Talking helped me figure out what I was thinking more than just being quiet and reading it."

"Exactly. So that tells me that part of your deeper comprehension was 'In Your Mind' and part of it was 'In Your Life.'"

Jen wrote on the chart paper under "In Your Mind":

You understand deeply when:
- Your beliefs are affirmed or strengthened (or changed) by something you read
- You feel like you're "behind" the character—a sense of advocacy, you want the best thing to happen to him/her

Then she wrote on the chart paper under "In Your Life":

You understand deeply when:
- You talk about what you understand with a partner or in the large group

"Tiffany, you really did both. You talked about how your existing beliefs were affirmed and strengthened. When you talked about the piece, your conversation reminded you that you have always believed that people who may not be beautiful or handsome have a lot of other great attributes. You talked about how you felt what we might call a sense of advocacy—that you wanted to speak out on the character's behalf in this piece. You were really behind her. But you went on to say something that I think is very important. You said that part of what you understood, you discovered only as you talked about it. That's really true for a lot of us as readers. We're not sure about all we think, feel, and believe until we speak to someone about it.

"You guys helped us understand, in part, how comprehension strategies help us understand more deeply. Tiffany, you made a connection, but what was most interesting is where the connection led you in your understanding. You didn't stop at making a connection. You went on to tell me how the connection helped you understand this text more deeply. It reminded you of beliefs and values you've already have, and it gave you a sense of advocating, mentally cheering for the character because of the strength you saw in her."

Jen heard from other students and found that restating their responses, then asking them to take their time and focus on where the comprehension strategy led them in their minds, was a useful way to get them to go deeper. (See the box "Jen's Lesson in a Nutshell" if you're ready to try this with your class.)

When a comprehension strategy leads us to understand the text in a new way, it may be an indicator of deeper understanding. I call these markers of deeper thinking the Outcomes of Understanding. In *To Understand* (2008), I introduced the Dimensions and Outcomes of Understanding, though the latter only briefly. Dimensions of Understanding (see Appendix C on the book's website) are observable behaviors that may indicate deep understanding. We can model and describe the dimensions and watch for them as students work. They serve as indicators that students may be understanding more deeply. Outcomes of Understanding, which I'll explore in much greater depth in this book, are cognitive markers of deeper understanding. I've revised these indicators significantly since the publication of *To Understand.*

When a comprehension strategy leads us to understand the text in a new way, it may be an indicator of deeper understanding. I call these markers of deeper thinking the Outcomes of Understanding.

> **Jen's lesson in a nutshell:** Try this with your students!

1. Jen began by describing what she believes is involved in deeper understanding and how she hopes the students will experience it.

2. She read aloud a short piece of text (an excerpt in this case) that was provocative and relevant.

3. She invited the students to read it silently, making notes about how they came to understand in their minds (by using certain comprehension strategies, e.g.) and in their lives (by underlining, writing notes, drawing arrows to connect different parts of the text, and/or talking with others).

4. She asked the students to share with a partner, focusing on how they came to understand.

5. She asked students to share what their partners had told them about their process of understanding.

6. She reacted to their initial responses by asking them how their strategy use helped them understand more deeply and by probing with the question, "What else?"

7. She recorded their responses on a chart under the headings "In My Mind" and "In My Life."

In Figure 1.2 (pages 18–19), items 6 and 9 in the left column describe where the use of a comprehension strategy actually led Tiffany. She was able to describe deeper understanding in her thinking. She used schema (a comprehension strategy), but when asked how that helped her understand the text better, she plumbed the depths more to talk about the affirmation of her beliefs and values and the sense of advocacy that she felt for the character. Now the question became: How could Jen encourage others to do the same and to do so consistently and independently?

As an observer of this lesson, I noticed that the key to getting Tiffany to a deeper level in her response was that Jen asked her, after she shared her use of a comprehension strategy, to talk about how the strategy led her to understand the text better—the outcome. When Jasmine and Tiffany shared a connection, for example, she pushed them further by asking, "How did the connection help you understand more deeply?" and then probing further by merely asking, "What else?" She restated what Tiffany said, giving her time to think more deeply about how she viewed the piece, and then captured her thinking in a concise way on an anchor chart.

Once we pass the threshold of believing that students—all students—are capable of thinking at high levels, we must focus on how to get them there.

Jen confessed later that, while she was pleased with the opening of her lesson—the statements in which she described how she views deeper understanding—she wasn't convinced that the lesson would lead to any significant changes in her students' reading. She couldn't have been more pleasantly surprised! Jen's students continued to rally that day. Her words inspired them. It seemed to matter a great deal that Jen believed they were capable of deeper thinking, and had articulated her hope for them. She had a nagging instinct that they could probe for further meaning, go deeper, remember, and reuse what they read. Jen was determined to herald a new day in her classroom, one in which students were expected to push their thinking further. She knew that theirs was only an initial conversation, but she hoped that their insights that day and in the days to come would be enough to launch them on a journey toward deeper understanding.

*****

Jen and her colleagues were wise, I believe, to ask, "What's next?" Once we pass the threshold of believing that students—all students—are capable of thinking at high levels, we must focus on how to get them there. It's not a matter of waiting and hoping that maybe, someday, they'll happen to utter an insightful response to a book—these are learned behaviors. We are in the fortunate position of getting to teach them to think more deeply and to remember more lastingly.

In the coming chapters, we'll focus on what that instruction looks like. But for now, I would like to propose that we need a new language to define and describe higher-level thinking as it relates to reading and responding. We can begin with the Outcomes of Understanding listed in Figure 1.2. We can then go further—we can invite our students, as Jen did, to participate in the conversation, to share their ideas about what it means to understand deeply. The chart Jen's students began that day can expand throughout the school year as students discover what they do in their minds and their lives to, in Jen's words, let books affect them in a profound way.

Outcomes of Understanding: Indicators of Deeper Comprehension

COGNITIVE OUTCOMES FOR READERS (Narrative Text)	COGNITIVE OUTCOMES FOR LEARNERS (Expository or Informational Text)
1. We **experience empathy**—we sense that we are somehow *in the book*. Empathy can include: • **Character empathy**, in which we feel we know the characters, experience the same emotions, stand by them in their trials. • **Setting empathy**, in which we feel a part of the setting. • **Conflict empathy**, in which we experience the internal and external conflict as if firsthand.	1. We **imagine ourselves in real-world situations, immersed in ideas**. We have compelling questions. We take on the role of scientist, social scientist, mathematician. • We begin to **understand thought leadership**—we explore and seek to understand the lives of those who have made significant contributions to a field and begin to imagine how we might do the same. • We **understand the problems that led to discoveries and new solutions** in the scientific, technological, or social scientific world. We have a sense of the elements that make a situation problematic and of the steps needed to solve the problem.
2. We **experience a memorable emotional response**—the sense that what we feel may be part of our emotional life for a long time.	2. We **experience a memorable emotional response.** We may feel a passion to learn more or compassion for others who are affected by a problem.
3. We **experience the aesthetic**—we find particular aspects of a book very compelling and feel a desire to linger with or reread portions of the text we find beautiful, well-written, surprising, humorous, or moving.	3. We **experience the aesthetic**—we feel a sense of wonder about the complexities and nuances related to a concept we are learning. We may feel compelled to reread portions and dig more deeply into the topic.
4. We **ponder**—we feel a desire to **pause and dwell** in new facets and twists in the text. We may want to reread in order to think more about certain ideas.	4. We **revisit and rethink**—we reread texts or explore new ones to learn more about a concept.
5. We find ourselves thinking about the book even when we're not reading. We **generate new ideas and imagine new possibilities** in characters' lives; our ideas are original, but related to the text.	5. We **generate our own hypotheses and theories** about why and how things happen in the natural and social world; we check our hypotheses against those that have been tested. We may feel moved to take action to mitigate a conflict in the world.
6. We **advocate and evaluate**—we may follow one character or plot element more intensively and may have the sense of being "behind" the character(s) or narrator. We want events to evolve in a particular way.	6. We **direct our energy to comprehending a few ideas of great import**. We develop a sense of what matters most, what is worth remembering, and have the confidence to focus on important ideas rather than on details unimportant to the larger text. We evaluate the information for credibility and bias.

Figure 1.2

Outcomes of Understanding: Indicators of Deeper Comprehension	
COGNITIVE OUTCOMES FOR READERS (Narrative Text)	**COGNITIVE OUTCOMES FOR LEARNERS** (Expository or Informational Text)
7. We **recognize patterns and symbols**. We may experience a moment of insight or begin to use our knowledge of literary tools to recognize themes and motifs as well as symbols and metaphors in stories.	7. We **recognize patterns and text structures**, including • **Cause/effect**—we use our background knowledge to discern how events affect one another. • **Comparisons and contrasts**—we develop a sense of how concepts are similar and different. • **Chronology**—we sense the general order of development or the progression of a series of ideas. • **Problem/solution**—when a problem is introduced, we begin to consider solutions and/or to anticipate solutions that may be presented in the text; we anticipate new problems and solutions related to earlier ones.
8. We **extrapolate** from details in the text and **arrive at global conclusions from focal points** in the text. These conclusions may reach beyond the scope of the text to other people, events, or settings; we may feel an urge to take action to solve a problem or to act on an issue in our community.	8. We **create schema**—we realize how newly learned concepts fit into our existing background knowledge and how we can make sense of new information in relation to what we already know. We determine whether our existing knowledge is accurate, inaccurate (and needs to be revised), or incomplete and look to a variety of sources to complete missing schema.
9. We **evaluate the author's intentions, values, and claims**. We actively study the author's style and may choose to replicate it in our writing; we are aware of how he/she manipulates our thinking with tools such as diction, foreshadowing, and metaphor. We sometimes argue with the author; we evaluate the author's success in making the book credible and we are attuned to ways in which he/she affirms or changes our **beliefs, values, and opinions**.	9. We **recognize the influence of beliefs, values, and opinions**. We may experience an affirmation of existing beliefs/values/opinions and/or sense newly developing ones related to the text and can give evidence to support them.
10. We **remember**. We develop the sense of permanence that comes with deeply understanding something; we know that we'll be able to apply ideas in new situations.	10. We **remember**. We develop the sense of permanence that comes with deeply understanding something; we know that we'll be able to apply concepts in new situations.

Figure 1.2 (continued)

Insights and Empathy

*What does it mean to comprehend
deeply in narrative text?*

When we understand deeply, we experience words and ideas that we find beautiful or compelling; we change our thinking, often reexamining our values and beliefs; we actually generate new thinking and ideas; we are occasionally inspired; and we remember and reuse what we have learned. Do you recall a book you read or an idea you learned when you understood deeply? Perhaps you were engaged in conversations with friends and you were able to articulate your point of view on an issue clearly and succinctly; maybe you read a book in which the character remained in your mind for days after you finished reading or you actually felt what the character felt. Have you ever chosen to read a difficult text or tackle a complex idea because you wanted to challenge yourself to understand something that seemed just beyond your grasp? Have you found yourself drawn to explore more extensively a question of passionate interest or read a text that challenges your point of view?

These questions point to what people—children and adults—experience when they understand deeply. I want our students to have these experiences regularly—I believe they are addictive in the most positive sense of the word. To understand deeply is to experience intellectual engagement that itself spawns more voracious learning, which leads to more lasting comprehension. It's a delicious cycle.

In this chapter, I propose a set of indicators or descriptors of deeper understanding in narrative text—markers we can be alert to in ourselves and our students. Here's the key: If we define and discuss these markers of deep understanding with students, children will exhibit them more consistently and across a wider range of topics and texts. We'll begin to see that students find intellectual engagement and deeper understanding intoxicating and will seek more such experiences. It is especially helpful if we have a discourse of deeper understanding for the classroom—terms and ideas that we use regularly to describe the experience of understanding deeply.

If we define and discuss these markers of deep understanding with students, children will exhibit them more consistently and across a wider range of topics and texts.

Deeper understanding often occurs within the context of comprehension strategy instruction and discussion about books—it's often lurking just beyond a child's use of a strategy, so we need to continue to teach comprehension strategies and to understand that they are powerful tools in leveraging deeper understanding. Comprehension strategy instruction is based on an instructional model in which teachers gradually release responsibility for using a strategy to students. For help in planning a comprehension strategy study, please see Appendix D on the book's website. When a child makes a connection, determines importance, infers, or synthesizes, she is using a tool to reach for deeper understanding, but we need, initially, to facilitate that reach if she is likely to understand deeply on her own. Comprehension strategies are the tools we give children to help them understand. There is more, though. If strategies are the tools to reach deeper understanding, what *is* deeper understanding?

As I described in Chapter 1, I have discovered twenty markers of deeper understanding (ten each for narrative and expository or informational text) that I call the Outcomes of Understanding. You'll notice that there is some overlap. Figure 2.1 opposite (half of Figure 1.2) is the collection of *narrative* outcomes. We'll discuss expository outcomes in Chapter 4.

These ten cognitive outcomes are, in my view, *descriptors* or *hallmarks* of deeper understanding in narrative text. The outcomes were gleaned from responses I've recorded from children and adults, usually when the reader was describing strategy use and discussing a book. In these interactions, the reader shared how he was thinking strategically, and I followed up by asking how his thinking helped him understand the piece he was reading better or what he understood in the piece because of his question, or connection, or inference—whatever strategy was used. I often asked the reader to take his time and think about what he now knows or believes about the text. There were usually moments of silence that were uncomfortable (mostly for the teacher) before the reader responded with an insight about the text. When he did, it was often the kind of response that we used to hear only occasionally—surprising, insightful, probing, fresh perspectives that led the entire group into a discussion of new facets of the text that they had not yet discovered. These responses fell into some very predictable patterns—and slowly, I realized these patterns were markers of deeper understanding. These became the Outcomes of Understanding.

For example, many readers described moments when they paused to think more about the text and found that they wanted to reread it in order to contemplate a particular aspect (Figure 2.1, outcome 4). Many others began by focusing on a detail in the text, but found that it led them to draw much larger conclusions about the world beyond the text (outcome 8).

I realized that, if a child was describing her thinking and it correlated to one of the outcomes, we could *reliably predict that she understood quite deeply*—that she was more likely to remember and reapply an idea from the text. She may or may not have understood as well elsewhere in the text, but when she described, for example, how she felt emotionally moved to take some kind of action to mitigate a problem in the world (outcome 8), I have little doubt that she understood the subtleties of the text. It soon became clear to me that I was describing some (perhaps not all, but at least some) of the hallmarks of higher-level comprehension.

Outcomes of Understanding in Narrative Text: Indicators of Deeper Comprehension

Cognitive Outcomes for Readers

1. We **experience empathy**—we sense that we are somehow *in the book*. Empathy can include:
   - **Character empathy**, in which we feel we know the characters, experience the same emotions, stand by them in their trials.
   - **Setting empathy**, in which we feel a part of the setting.
   - **Conflict empathy**, in which we experience the internal and external conflict as if firsthand.

2. We **experience a memorable emotional response**—the sense that what we feel may be part of our emotional life for a long time.

3. We **experience the aesthetic**—we find particular aspects of a book very compelling and feel a desire to linger with or reread portions of the text we find beautiful, well-written, surprising, humorous, or moving.

4. We **ponder**—we feel a desire to **pause and dwell** in new facets and twists in the text. We may want to reread in order to think more about certain ideas.

5. We find ourselves thinking about the book even when we're not reading. We **generate new ideas and imagine new possibilities** in characters' lives; our ideas are original, but related to the text.

6. We **advocate and evaluate**—we may follow one character or plot element more intensively and may have the sense of being "behind" the character(s) or narrator. We want events to evolve in a particular way.

7. We **recognize patterns and symbols**. We may experience a moment of insight or begin to use our knowledge of literary tools to recognize themes and motifs as well as symbols and metaphors in stories.

8. We **extrapolate** from details in the text and **arrive at global conclusions from focal points** in the text. These conclusions may reach beyond the scope of the text to other people, events, or settings; we may feel an urge to take action to solve a problem or to act on an issue in our community.

9. We **evaluate the author's intentions, values, and claims**. We actively study the author's style and may choose to replicate it in our writing; we are aware of how he/she manipulates our thinking with tools such as diction, foreshadowing, and metaphor. We sometimes argue with the author; we evaluate the author's success in making the book credible and we are attuned to ways in which he/she affirms or changes our **beliefs, values, and opinions**.

10. We **remember**. We develop the sense of permanence that comes with deeply understanding something; we know that we'll be able to apply ideas in new situations.

Figure 2.1

A second grader named Ella shared an inference about the book *One Green Apple* by Eve Bunting. I asked, "What else do you understand in this book because you inferred?" She paused for a moment before continuing and then said, "I guess when I had that inference it made me think about the girl with the scarf [worn as a religious symbol] when no one else had one. She didn't have any English and she was trying so hard to fit in with what everyone else was doing. When I read that part, my heart started beating really hard, just like if I was her and I didn't know how to use the apple machine and my hands were shaking. I guess I felt like I *was* her and the things that were happening to her were really happening to me." That comment describes *empathy* for the character (the first outcome in Figure 2.1). Feeling as if you are actually *in* the book, responding as the characters might, and experiencing their conflicts as your own is an empathetic response—one of the hallmarks of deeper understanding.

Empathy is just one of the outcomes I've noticed. Children may begin, for example, by describing a question they had while reading; then after I ask how their question helped them better understand the text, they go on to say how they found a particular part of the text dense enough with meaning that it was worthy of a second or third reading (see Figure 2.1, outcome 4). Many of the adults and children with whom I've worked describe a desire to slow down and consider what may be layered underneath the words; they sense that there is something more to understand and feel compelled to stop reading and consider the ideas that are not as obvious upon first reading. That process of rethinking and seeking new insights is also an Outcome of Understanding.

Weaving the Outcomes into Our Work with Students

The question of how to weave the outcomes into our work with children is an open one. I have introduced the outcomes directly through a think-aloud and have "caught a child in the act" of using an outcome and pointed it out to her and/or the whole class. I don't believe there is a right or wrong way to teach or discuss the outcomes in classrooms—I look forward to your ideas about how to do so—but I will show, in the video that accompanies the next chapter, one way to approach it.

I've noted the outcomes in a wide range of grade levels. For example, I was reading Mem Fox's classic book *Wilfrid Gordon McDonald Partridge* to a first-grade class. The book tells the story a young man (the title character) who visits a home for the elderly and helps them recall certain memories using different objects, such as a shell. I was focusing my lesson on images and asked the children to turn and talk about images they might have had as I read. I couldn't help but hear Katie, who had barely finished rotating her body to face Luke when she said, "We gotta get over there, right now!" When Luke looked puzzled, she went on, "You know there is a place where old people live right down that way." She pointed toward the window. "If we went down there and helped them, we could get them their memories back. We should go over there!" Katie's image led her to experience an emotional response and she found herself compelled to take action to mitigate a problem in her world (Figure 2.1, outcome 8). Following the turn-and-talk, I told the rest of the class about Katie's insight.

"An extraordinary thing happened while you were talking to each other," I said in a hushed voice. "It happened to Katie and I want to tell all of you about it because if you think about it a little, it may happen to you as well. While I was reading *Wilfrid Gordon McDonald Partridge*, Katie had an image of the home for the elderly right down this street, and in her image she saw people who may, just like the people in this story, have lost their memories." Hands shot up around the room. Others had obviously had the same image. "But wait," I said, giving the silent signal to put hands down. "Something else really important happened! Katie had the image, but then she had a feeling so deep in her heart—it's called an emotion—a feeling that was so strong that it made her want very much to help the people at the home for the elderly. Sometimes when your heart aches or is filled with joy or you feel very strongly about something, it makes you want to take action—it makes you want to do something to make the world a better place, and today that happened to Katie!"

I've witnessed dozens of similar reactions in which children find their emotional responses to a text so overwhelming that they feel compelled to take some kind of action. I believe when we see responses like Katie's, reactions that reflect any of the outcomes, we're seeing deeper understanding, and I believe we ought to define and describe it to children. The Outcomes of Understanding give us a language to do just that.

> "Sometimes when your heart aches or is filled with joy or you feel very strongly about something, it makes you want to take action—it makes you want to do something to make the world a better place, and today that happened to Katie!"

Your Turn

If we are going to define and describe the characteristics of deeper understanding for children, we must be able to do so for ourselves. Please read the following essay, "Remembering All the Boys," which comes from a wonderful collection entitled *This I Believe*. As you read the essay, take notes about how you come to understand. Do you use comprehension strategies? If so, which ones? Try to pay attention to the ways your mind works when you are trying to make sense of text for the first time.

If we are going to define and describe the characteristics of deeper understanding for children, we must be able to do so for ourselves.

Remembering All the Boys

I believe that everyone deserves flowers on their grave.

When I go to the cemetery to visit my brother, it makes me sad to see graves—just cold stones—and no flowers on them.

They look lonely, like nobody loves them. I believe this is the worst thing in the world—that loneliness. No one to visit you and brush off the dust from your name and cover you with color. A grave without any flowers looks like the person has been forgotten. And then what was the point of even living—to be forgotten?

Almost every day my brother's grave has something new on it: flowers from me, or candles from the Dollar Store, or an image of the Virgin Maria, or shot glasses. There's even some little Homies, these little toys that look like gangsters.

Once my brother's homies even put a bunch of marijuana on there for him—I think my mother took it away. I think she also took away the blue rag someone put there for him one day.

Sometimes, when I bring flowers, I fix the flowers on the graves around my brother's grave. Some of the headstones have birthdates near my brother's; they are young, too. But many of them, if they have any little toys or things on them, those are red.

All around my brother are boys who grew up to like red, making them the enemies of my brother. My brother was sixteen when he was shot by someone who liked red, who killed him because he liked blue. And when I go to the cemetery, I put flowers on the graves of the boys who liked red, too.

Sometimes I go to the cemetery with one of my best friends, who had a crush on a boy who liked blue. And we will go together and bring a big bunch of flowers, enough for both of these boys whose families are actually even from the same state in Mexico.

There is no one but me and a few of my friends who go to both graves. Some people think it's a bad idea. Some people think it's heroic.

I think they're both being silly. I don't go to try to disrespect some special rules or stop any kind of war. I go because I believe that no matter where you came from or what you believed in, when you die, you want flowers on your grave and people who visit you and remember you that way.

I'm not any kind of traitor or any kind of hero. I am the sister of Rogelio Bautista and I say his name so you will hear it and be one more person who remembers him. I want everyone to remember all the boys, red and blue, in my cemetery. When we remember, we put flowers on their graves.

—FROM ELVIA BAUTISTA, *THIS I BELIEVE*

Reread the essay, taking more notes about the cognitive processes you used to understand. Now ask yourself this question: In what ways do the processes I've just used help me understand this essay better? For example, if you noticed that you asked several questions as you read, how did those questions help you understand more effectively? What do you know or understand about this piece that you might not have understood had you not asked those questions? When you've answered that question, look at Figure 2.1. Do you notice that your questions, for example, led you to find empathy with the character (outcome 1)? Did you perhaps find yourself advocating for the character, pulling for her when she left flowers on the gravesites of both rival gangs (outcome 6)? Did you notice that your own beliefs and values influenced your understanding in any way (outcome 9)? You have just defined and described your deeper comprehension. A comprehension strategy such as questioning *led to* deeper understanding in the form of empathy, advocacy, and values examination!

I recall working with a group of teachers outside Cincinnati, Ohio, at the annual Lakota VIEW literacy conference, a wonderful event that draws teachers from all over the country. I had just read this essay aloud to them and just as you have done, I asked the teachers to take some notes as they read the piece to themselves. I wanted them to focus on how they came to understand the essay—what was going on in their minds. If, as is usually the case, they found that they used comprehension strategies to understand the piece, I was eager to show that those strategies can *lead* to something more, a deeper layer of understanding, if we give some time and thought to the process.

After asking the teachers to share their insights with each other for a few minutes, I asked for someone to share what their *partner* had said— something surprising or provocative or useful—rather than sharing what they had said to their partner. This is a process I use with children to ensure that they are really listening to each other when they turn and talk.

One teacher raised her hand and said that her partner had schema for the piece—a connection to background knowledge. She emphasized that her partner had no schema for gangs, but did think about her grandmother's grave as she was reading the piece. She had an image of her grandmother's grave standing alone without flowers or other mementos. A sigh of recognition spread around the room. Many, it seems, had similar connections and visual images. I wanted, though, to know if the partner's understanding went deeper, so I turned and asked her how, if at all, her schematic connections and images had helped her better understand the piece.

She paused for a moment and said, "Well, at the beginning I was thinking about how unconnected this essay was to my life. I don't have any connections to gangs, I don't know anyone who does; I hate the influence that gangs have on kids. But thinking about my grandmother's grave sort of humanized this whole essay. It made me think about a relatively small part of life—remembering to adorn the graves of your loved ones—and how it really is such a big, universal thing. Honoring the dead, I mean it crosses all cultures and age groups. This little thing—remembering to put flowers on a grave—it made me think of much bigger issues like how we have loss in common. We all lose people we love. This essay made me think of the waste of potential in those kids who died, but it also gave me this common bond with the sister—we are all walking around with loss."

This teacher was strategic as she read (making schematic connections and creating images), but her connections and images led her (led all of us) to much deeper understanding. She took small or *focal* examples and extrapolated to a *global* (or universal) issue (see Figure 2.1, outcome 8). The simple eloquence of her remarks gave everyone pause. She extrapolated from the details in the text and in so doing caused most of the rest of those present to think more deeply, perhaps in a way that had not before.

Let me pause for a moment and ask you to go back to the essay, "Remembering All the Boys." Reread the essay, noting your responses in the margins. Ask yourself the key question—how did my strategic thinking help me to understand this piece more deeply or effectively? Or, reflect on this question: What do I understand because of my strategic thinking that I might have missed without it? Look over the list of Outcomes of Understanding to see if you recognize any of them in your own reading. To be clear, this is likely not a definitive list. I may well have missed some patterns of thinking that should be outcomes, and there is certainly a great deal of overlap among these markers. But I imagine, if you give yourself the time, you too will notice that you're thinking about one or more of these outcomes, especially when you pause during reading or when you are reading a second or third time. This experience is deeper understanding.

*****

I want students to have that same experience, and I believe that they can. If we are aware enough of our own thinking, we can define and describe our experiences to children. If we aren't conscious of our strategic thinking and the resultant outcomes, however, it's going to be very difficult to describe them to children. We can make an enormous difference in our teaching if we read and consciously attend, not only to our strategy use, but also to the Outcomes of Understanding.

CHAPTER

3

From the Inside

*Integrating strategy instruction
and narrative outcomes*

I love nothing more than gathering around a table with teachers and other school leaders working to lay out a blueprint for growth. I have come to appreciate the complexity of change as well as the interplay between a school plotting its own path and the district's crucial role in supporting change. When I have an opportunity to take visitors to schools like James Lewis Elementary in Blue Springs, Missouri, where I've consulted for a number of years, we inevitably find ourselves trying to reconstruct and define the school's progress, describing the components that have been critical to its ongoing success. It's hard to pin down—what makes a faculty come together, align their beliefs, and orient their practices so that they are truly responsive to children's learning needs? The conversations in which we try to unpack these successes and make them applicable to others are very challenging, but it is deeply satisfying to be part of a school or district team, thinking into the future about literacy instruction and, years later, being able to study teachers who have made extraordinary changes in their practice.

I'm fascinated by the change process, yet I often read and write about schools and districts that have already made significant improvements, that are in the later stages of this process, thus making it more difficult to understand how they got there. In fact, many of our field's most popular books and videos paint a picture of the "best of the best." We read about teachers who have experienced extensive professional learning, who have spent years studying best practices and are at the pinnacle of their work in literacy. Many of the teachers I describe elsewhere in this book fit this description.

For that reason, I want to examine a school that is more representative of many American schools. It is a school on the cusp of significant change. I believe it will be instructive to look at this school early in its change process, when teachers are beginning to transform literacy instruction from a more traditional model to the kind of instruction we all want for children. In this chapter as well as in Chapters 5 and 7, we'll look at this school *from the inside* through text and video. My hope in each of these chapters is to zoom in on one school, one classroom, one lesson that is one illustration of the new generation of comprehension instruction. In each of these chapters, we'll visit Kolmar Elementary, situated about thirty miles southwest of Chicago in Midlothian, Illinois, and look in on a different grade level.

Kolmar Elementary is relatively new to a reader's/writer's workshop (Literacy Studio) model and comprehension strategy instruction. In-depth professional learning is in the early stages and teachers' attitudes range from excited and ready to learn to more skeptical about making change. The school draws a diverse population of children; many don't come to school with the background knowledge and early learning experiences we would hope would be available for all children. Many speak English as their second language, some live in poverty, and some have had to endure situations no child should ever have to experience.

There are promising signs at Kolmar, however. The school has a very strong principal, Cathy Thompson, and the teachers, many of whom are early-career teachers, care deeply about students and are working tirelessly to reach them in the most effective ways possible. Assistant superintendent Carrie Cahill, a visionary and knowledgeable leader, has initiated Saturday morning study groups in which she sits down with teachers from around the district to discuss new professional books and think together about implications for their classrooms. She is committed, though resources are extremely scarce, to providing site-based professional learning opportunities and is nurturing literacy coaches' work in the district. There is progress, but all recognize that much learning lies ahead of them.

The lesson we'll scrutinize in this chapter and through the accompanying DVD took place in a second-grade classroom at Kolmar. Kelly Young's children streamed into the classroom that morning, as do kids in thousands of schools. Some were brimming with stories to share; others hadn't had enough sleep the night before; some were sick; some may have been hungry. They were American children in an American school on a crisp, cloudy day in October.

Beginning with the Outcomes in Mind

▶ **STRATEGY:** Schema (extending schema from content in a book)

▶ **OUTCOMES:** Empathy and advocacy

Kelly had focused instruction on using relevant background knowledge—schema—for several weeks prior to the lesson I taught that day. My first objective was to encourage the children to move beyond thinking of schema as making "text-to-text," "text-to-self," and "text-to-world" connections, to go a little deeper in their thinking. I wanted to emphasize the critical need to **create new schema and extend and expand existing schema** as they encountered new content. I wanted them to go beyond looking for connections to their own lives—I wanted them to learn to *add* new information to their existing schema, thus understanding the book more deeply and lastingly.

I used Eve Bunting's book *One Green Apple* knowing that, embedded in the beautiful story, there would be new content related to a young Muslim girl's immigration to America and the trials she faced because she didn't speak English and dressed in traditional Muslim clothing. I wanted to show how we add new information to existing schema, but I also planned to be on the lookout for children's responses that indicated their **empathy** with or **advocacy** for the character—two of the Outcomes of Understanding discussed in Chapter 2. I certainly couldn't predict with certainty that either of these outcomes would emerge from what the students shared, but I planned to capitalize on the times I paused to think aloud to focus my own words on extending existing schema *and* on the outcomes of empathy and advocacy. Keeping any of the outcomes we discussed in Chapter 2 in mind from the beginning of a lesson helps me to ensure that my think-alouds will take the children more deeply into the meanings of the text without telling them *what* to think. They may or may not experience the same outcomes, but keeping them in mind helps me to deepen my think-alouds.

You'll remember that when a reader experiences empathy, he senses that he is somehow *in the book*. Empathy can include **character empathy**, in which we feel we know the characters and may experience the same emotions. It can also include **setting empathy**, in which we feel a part of the setting, and **conflict empathy**, in which we experience the characters' internal and external conflicts as if firsthand.

I also sensed that the children might find themselves **advocating** for the protagonist and **evaluating the actions** of other characters in the story. Advocacy implies that a reader may follow one character or plot element more intensively and may have the sense of being "behind" the character, wanting events to evolve in a particular way.

Strategies and Outcomes in Action

▶ *If you are watching the video, view **Schema, Segment 1**, now.*

At the beginning of the lesson, I acknowledged that the children had been studying schema for some time and made sure that they knew the lesson would begin with me sharing my thinking followed by them sharing their thinking. I asked them to tell me what they already knew about schema—their "schema for schema," as it were! Dejae began by sharing that schema is background knowledge. Travis added the word *connections* and got right to the heart of my objective when he said, "If you add something more to it, it's schema. It's a little about connections—it turns into schema when you add more to it." I was, of course, delighted to hear this and mentioned that Travis' idea is exactly what we would be talking about today in the read-aloud.

Ashanti added that if you have something in common with the character in the book, it can be sort of a connection. I pushed her a bit, sensing that she might be referring to empathy and sure enough, she said, "It [schema] helps you understand a book because . . . you know how the character feels if they have the best day ever."

▶ *If you are watching the video, view* **Schema, Segment 2**, *now.*

I told the students that today we were going to add to what they know about schema and that I was going to read Eve Bunting's wonderful book *One Green Apple*. I wanted to build schema about the text content early so they could focus on the more inferential aspects of the text, so I said in part, "In order to understand this book better, I'm going to use what I already know, have heard, and feel about moving from another country to another. I know that the girl in the book moved to a new country, and therefore moved to a new school."

I read a bit of the book and paused to think aloud, to build more schema. I said, in part, "My schema also tells me that the girl in this book is Muslim. I realize that our country has been at war with Muslim countries like Iraq and Afghanistan. I worry that this girl has had to live in war for some time because if she is coming from one of the countries that the U.S. doesn't get along with, she may have been living in the middle of a war. My schema tells me that to live in war means that people may have to leave their homes and live as refugees. My schema . . . tells me that people may come home to find their homes ruined, obliterated. My schema tells me that is what war is like and . . . that I don't want any child to ever live in a place where there is war. My schema helps me understand the life this girl may have lived before the book began."

▶ *If you are watching the video, view* **Schema, Segment 3**, *now.*

I read a bit more of the book, including a description of how the character felt "tight inside myself," and paused to think aloud about a situation in which I was speaking to a large group of people and felt tight inside myself, overwhelmed. I mentioned that my schema "helps me understand Farrah [the character] better. When I think about times when I've been so overwhelmed and not sure of myself, afraid that I'll make a mistake, I understand how she feels because I've felt the same thing."

Of course, I was beginning, in this think-aloud, to reveal my own empathy for the character. I wanted to probe more deeply than saying something like, "I have seen Muslim women who wear *dupattas* to cover their heads." I wanted to go straight to the emotional level, the pulse of this book. I wanted them to begin to imagine what it would

be like to find oneself in a new country, not speaking the language and dressing differently than those around you.

Before long, I noticed that Michael looked like he wanted to share something, but when I asked him, he demurred. I suggested that while I read another page, he pay attention to the schema he had and the new schema he was beginning to have. When I finished, he said, "It helps me understand the book because I know how the character feels when she moves to a new place . . . I moved to Midlothian."

I reflected back to him, "You know what it's like to . . . go to a new school. What else do you understand that helps you understand how the character feels?"

"You don't really feel comfortable in the new neighborhood until you stay there for a while, until you get to know it," Michael replied.

I restated what he had said again and asked, "How does it help you understand Farrah?"

"I know how she feels."

"Do I understand this correctly, Michael? You actually understand in your own heart what she might be feeling in her heart?"

There was a long pause. I tried again. "Can you feel what she feels?"

"Yeah."

There it was. Michael had shown that he went beyond a simple connection to understanding how the character felt because of the connection he made. I saw this as an opportunity to teach the outcome, to label what Michael had described and make it accessible to the rest of the children.

"Ladies and gentlemen," I began, "the most extraordinary thing has happened. Michael not only had a connection. He knows what it's like to move to a new school. He actually felt the way Farrah must feel. He has shown us that you can feel in your heart what the character feels in her heart. I just wonder," I said, rising to go to the easel. "Do you want to know what that is called? There's a word for what Michael did. Michael, you did something that even grown-up readers try their whole lives to do—the rest of you should look at this word." I wrote the word *empathy* on chart paper. "It may be that sometime soon you'll do what Michael did."

Travis pushed the discussion along when he suggested that Farrah might actually be happy to be in a new country to be away from "war and all that stuff." It was the first hint that the children were thinking about the bigger issues that underlie this book. Travis' comment hinted at another outcome, extrapolating from focal to global (Figure 1.2, outcome 8), but I decided to keep our focus on empathy and creating new schema—my tendency is to crowd too much into a lesson. I tried to show some restraint here!

In this lesson, I introduced empathy when a student demonstrated it as opposed to introducing it as a vocabulary word: "Okay, kids, here's this word *empathy*; here's what it means." One among them had already exhibited the outcome; all I had to do was name it and show them the word. I know that they will need many more explanations and examples of the various types of empathy before they fully integrate it into their working vocabulary and completely understand what it means, but Michael gave us the way in to a tool they can all use to understand more deeply. My challenge is to be attuned to the moments when children exhibit the outcome and to label it so that others can use the concept as well.

▶ *If you are watching the video, view* **Schema, Segment 4**, *now.*

Several other children shared connections, most of which didn't go beyond the simple "this happened to me, too" level, so I asked them to just spend a moment in silence "listening to the voice inside your mind that talks to you when you read." I wanted to take a breather from everyone trying to share their connections and just let them think about their schema. I waited a brief moment—too brief, I realize as I review the video—and let the silence engulf us. I began to read aloud again.

When I paused again to think aloud and to see what they were thinking, Nicholas said something that, frankly, I didn't think would lead us anywhere. I couldn't have been more wrong.

"On the part where they included Farrah in making the apple juice, I have a connection at Chuck E. Cheese. I included him [another child] to take that little sketch picture thing [an activity at the restaurant]."

I replied, "How does that help you understand Farrah?"

"I know how she feels."

"Say more."

"She feels happy because they were working together." I was delighted with this response and resisted the temptation to say, "Great job!"

"Say more."

"It's also—" Nicholas paused for a long time. "I need some time to think."

"That's really smart."

"It helps me understand the book because I know how her and the other kids feel."

"You had empathy! I'm so glad we waited while you thought because it made me think of this book in a completely different way." I restated his response and used the word *empathy* a couple more times so that everyone would associate it with Nicholas' response.

▶ *If you are watching the video, view **Schema, Segment 5**, now.*

At this point in the lesson, I was pleased that the children had shared connections and even empathy, but I was aware that my other objective—extending and expanding existing schema from the content of the book—was as yet unexplored. I asked, "I'm just curious if any child has new schema—not something that has happened to you before, but something that is new in your mind because you read this book."

The result was not what I had hoped. Trey told the class that he had come to Midlothian from Tennessee and "talked Southern and kids were laughing at me and I didn't even know" and then shared that "she came from Muslim and . . . she didn't really know how to speak English and I didn't know how to speak real English; I only knew how to talk Southern." I pointed out to the children that Trey had new schema because he realized that Farrah's head covering indicated that she was Muslim. Trey made a connection, but didn't indicate whether the connection had helped him understand the text more thoroughly. In retrospect, I should have pushed further. I wish that I had asked him how his experience helped him understand the story better.

In a portion you won't see on the video, Kylie and Ashanti shared their connections. I began to realize just how tough it is to help students move beyond sharing their experiences to really building new schema. I should have thought of this before, but finally realized that I was asking them to do something—share new schema from the book—that I hadn't yet modeled! How many times do I have to remind myself? If we're asking kids to engage in a new kind of thinking, we have to first think aloud to show them how!

▶ *If you are watching the video, view **Schema, Segment 6**, now.*

I tried to redeem myself at the end of the lesson. "It seems to me that I have some new things in my background knowledge or schema. I knew that Farrah came from a Muslim country, but now I understand that she has a lot of emotions about her move. She feels left out because she can't yet speak English with everyone; things like a school field trip are totally new to her; she senses that her teacher may be treating her as if she were stupid rather than just unable to understand the words; and finally she's relieved to be part of making the apple juice and saying her first words in English. These are new pieces in my schema; new things to think

about and add to what I already knew. Today in your reading, I'd like for you to think about *new schema,* what you're adding to your background knowledge. You may first find yourself thinking about a connection to yourself, but then think about what you've added to your knowledge. When we share later on, I'll be eager to hear from readers who know that they have added new schema to what they already knew.

"I also want to remind you that a lot of you had background knowledge for what Farrah was feeling. When you can think in your heart how it feels to be another person, you're feeling *empathy*—empathy is part of how you understand books better. There are times when you can stop in the book and think about what it's like—when you're reading today, it's really important that you think about your background knowledge, and empathy. See if you have empathy for the character."

As the children scrambled off to their independent reading, I reminded myself that we had discussed a lot of new content that day. I had certainly begun the conversation related to two of the objectives I outlined earlier, but I was fully aware that Kelly, their lucky teacher, would have to do a lot more thinking aloud and modeling before they would genuinely begin to integrate the new mental moves into their repertoire. I thought about how different it is to teach children to think rather than to merely recall and retell. Many years ago, I wouldn't have considered teaching two such abstract concepts to second graders and if I had, I probably would have done so in a lesson or two and wondered why they didn't "get it." When we're teaching children to be strategic readers, we're teaching them tools that will apply to most of the text they read—forever! I want them to be acutely aware when they add to existing schema in fiction and informational text and I certainly hope that they become so engaged in reading that they feel empathy for characters and others in the real world. I reminded myself that such vital thinking processes need to be taught in an in-depth manner, over a long period of time, and we must encourage children to apply them in a variety of texts and contexts.

Strategies and Outcomes in Action—A Conference

▶ *If you are watching the video, view **Conference with Ashanti** now.*

Ashanti's bright eyes and high level of engagement caught my eye during the crafting session (large-group instruction in the "craft" of reading and writing; see Appendix A on the website, www.heinemann.com/products/E02839.aspx, for a complete description of the Literacy Studio, or reader's/writer's workshop), and I thought she was understanding well. When I told Kelly I would be happy to confer with the children she was most

concerned about, I was surprised to learn that Ashanti was first on her list. In the conference, I wanted to focus on empathy and new schema; my goal was to provide immediate, tailored instruction within the context of Ashanti's book, *Thank You, Mr. Falker,* by Patricia Polacco. During the crafting session, she had been eager to share, but had mostly focused on personal (text-to-self) connections. When I sat down, Ashanti immediately began to read aloud. I have found that many children have the expectation that, in a conference, you always read aloud. Certainly, asking a child to read aloud is one way to understand them as a reader—how do they tackle unknown words, are they reading fluently—but I stopped her rather quickly because my goal for the conference was to focus on her thinking about her book—specifically, whether she could add new schema and/or experience empathy.

When I asked her to talk about her schema, especially new schema so far in the book, I was stunned by what she said. "I have new and old schema—when I first look at this page, it gave me chills . . . she [the character] kept staying at the same stage and I stayed at the same stage in reading and she began to feel dumb. I felt that when I was in a different school. I felt I was the only one who couldn't read—I felt dumb."

I wanted, of course, to reassure her, to tell her she's not dumb, but I got another message from Ashanti. She was very matter-of-fact in recalling her other life as a reader. This business of feeling dumb was in the past. It related to her life, but that was another chapter for her, a time before Kolmar Elementary, a time when she was "staged"—leveled, I presume—with respect to the rest of the class rather than being taught as an individual reader. I sensed that her experience in the other school was based on someone classifying her rather than addressing her specific learning needs. It reinforced for me how potent the labeling of children is, how clearly they understand when they are in a lower level or not moving through the "stages" in the same way others are and how their reaction sticks with them. I was so grateful that Ashanti wound up at Kolmar.

"How did it help you understand the book better?" I asked.

Ashanti's reply: "It helped me understand the book better because I knew how she felt—sad, alone, and jealous."

"You were empathetic . . . You were saying that you felt sad, alone, and jealous and that helped you understand Tricia in the book. Is there any new schema? Is there something that will be part of your thinking from now on, but it wasn't part of your schema before you read this book?" In that moment, I tried to decide whether I wanted to focus on her empathy for the character or whether I wanted to push her to think about adding new schema to existing schema.

Ashanti, of course, led the way. "Before when she [the teacher] read this book, I fell in love with this book. That week she kept reading this book and I was just in love with this book . . . "

I realized that she was particularly drawn to the book because it tells the author's own story as a struggling reader. I decided to broaden her ideas about what schema is and can do for us——I would teach her about a new type of schema, a concept that had yet to be introduced to the class. In retrospect, I realize that if I had decided to emphasize empathy in the conference, it would have been equally successful.

"Ashanti," I said, "You have new schema—you have author schema—you know about the way a particular author writes. You know something about the kind of books and the way a particular author writes. You can say Patricia Polacco writes this kind of book, a particular kind of book. You can say you have *author schema.*" Ashanti's response was gorgeous.

"Really?" she asked, eyes wide.

"Yes, and I think you're the first kid in this whole room to do that! Let's think about author schema. Today I read a book by Eve Bunting—what do you know about Eve Bunting as an author?"

At that point, Ashanti essentially retold the story and didn't seem to understand that having author schema is having an idea about the kinds of writing an author does and her propensities, her preferences, and the topics toward which she gravitates.

This time, I remembered to think aloud before I expected Ashanti to really understand this new concept. "Let's talk for a second about my author schema for Eve Bunting. Eve Bunting writes about difficult, challenging, hard things that happen in people's lives—if you knew that one of the things she likes to do as an author, that one of the things she likes to do is write about times when it's hard for people in their lives, then you could say that you had author schema for Eve Bunting.

"Now, when you're thinking about Eve Bunting, what do you know about the kinds of books she likes to write?"

Ashanti answered, though now her focus was on *Thank You, Mr. Falker.* "I know that she likes to help people to understand how not to be mean to other people—you should be nice to new people and not be rude." Now we were getting somewhere.

It was time to leave Ashanti with something new to work on, a challenge to continue to apply what we had discussed in the conference. I asked her to read three Patricia Polacco books and to be prepared to tell the other kids what kind of author she is—to be able to share her author schema and tell the rest of the class what it means to have author schema. I know that by building more experience with this author, Ashanti will gradually begin to develop a sense of what Polacco is trying to do in her books, what she hopes readers will take away with them. That's author schema, and if Ashanti can be the one who teaches the rest of her class about it, so much the better. They will undoubtedly remember her lesson as much or more than mine or their teacher's. And in asking Ashanti to take the reins on the lesson about author schema, I know that the small voice—diminishing, but still present—that tells her she might not be at the right "stage" or that she might be dumb will be silenced.

Ashanti responded, as you might imagine, with, "Yea!" She was jazzed and ready to go. I left the conference wishing that I was Ashanti's second-grade teacher.

Looking Back

Planning for long-term school change often begins with a group of educators gathered around a table with chart paper and markers nearby. I love the roll-up-your-sleeves spirit in that kind of discussion, but as I look at schools like Kolmar Elementary in Midlothian, Illinois, I am reminded how much of the real "stuff" of school change isn't ever captured on chart paper. Real school change happens every day in every classroom and is shaped by individual teachers who are cognizant of their beliefs, knowledgeable about reading theory and research, and able to use that knowledge to inform minute-by-minute decisions in interactions with children. Decisions like pausing to give Nicholas time to think and how to push Ashanti forward in a conference are based not only on what the child needs, but also on understanding what each strategy entails—the key ideas that we can weave into each strategy study (see Appendix B, "Comprehension Strategies Defined," on the book's website), the Outcomes of Understanding—and on our beliefs and the direction the school and district have outlined. We bring a convergence of understanding to every moment we interact with children.

Based on our discussions in Chapter 2 and 3, I'd like to pose one more question: Do we consistently embed our highest expectations about children's capacity for deeper understanding in those decisions? If you have a sense that your students can push their thinking to deeper levels, pay attention to that instinct!

We can begin by listening intently to what children are telling us when they say, "I felt just like that," or "She likes to write books about how not to be mean and rude to each other." Aren't those statements really saying, "I feel empathy" and "I'm capable of doing much more than making a text-to-self connection"? When I reviewed my notes and video footage before beginning this book and extracted the patterns in children's thinking I now call the Outcomes of Understanding, it was children like Nicholas and Ashanti I had in mind. But, we have to listen to what children are *really* saying. If we can label and describe their initial attempts—I felt just like she did—with language they can apply on their own—the term *empathy*, for example—we are leaving them with the tools to think more deeply, more consistently, and independently. We are leaving them with a language that just might last a lifetime.

CHAPTER

4

Immersed in Ideas

What does it mean to comprehend deeply in informational text?

Walking between classrooms, I get a vivid sense of the children who interact and work at James Lewis Elementary in Blue Springs, Missouri. The hallways are adorned with photographs of children, their writing and art, and their thinking about books. Sounds of children conversing about books drift from the classrooms. Their work is valued, their interests and passions celebrated— a visitor encounters visible and audible evidence of the efficacy children must feel in this school. Each grade level has created its own little reading area in the hallways where children from any classroom can escape to read under the soft light of a lamp, meet with their book club, or practice reading with a senior citizen who volunteers in the school. There are also intimate spaces in which to read and talk in every classroom. I have to remind myself that I'm in a classroom, not a cozy den in someone's home.

In Chapter 2, we looked at the indicators that children are thinking deeply in narrative text. Now I want to visit this extraordinary school to look at the indicators—the Outcomes of Understanding—that show that children are thinking more deeply in *informational*, or *nonfiction*, texts. For the purposes of this book, I'll use the term *informational* to refer to text that contains factual information, even if it is presented in a narrative format. I have observed that these indicators are slightly different in informational text, although there are some clear overlaps with narrative fiction.

When thinking about the markers that show that children understand deeply in informational text, we have to consider the degree to which students are actually learning—retaining and reapplying—the concepts about which they read. Do they actually recall and reuse learned concepts in new contexts, or are they only putting that new information in short-term memory, where it will fade within weeks? Are they manipulating their thinking to link newly learned information to prior knowledge, or schema, on the topic? Do they realize how schema changes when you learn something new? Do students immerse themselves in a variety of texts, answering questions of passionate interest? Are they reading texts from the point of view of a scientist or social scientist, artist, musician, athlete, or other real-world role? Are they generating hypotheses about how and why things happen? Are they focused on the ideas that are most important? Do they have a sense that they need to rethink previously held beliefs in order to accommodate new information? These are some of the Outcomes of Understanding (see Figure 4.1) in informational text. To explore them a bit further, let's visit James Lewis Elementary and then zoom in on a conference with a fourth grader there.

Schools like James Lewis remind me that there are physical manifestations of the Outcomes of Understanding—of deep comprehension. Here, there are records of children's thinking about books everywhere you look.

In one classroom I notice a chart in the children's own writing that lists questions about the books students are reading in one column and comments about how those questions helped them better understand the books in the second column. In another classroom, the teacher has recorded examples of children's inferences from poetry, historical fiction, and realistic fiction showing how readers infer differently in different genres. In another, the teachers and children are working on a chart titled "How do we understand?"

The classrooms and public spaces at James Lewis are extraordinary—they make me want to grab a book and join the children who are deeply engaged in reading, thinking, and discussing. More intriguing to me, however, are the *invisible* components of this school's success story—a story that is mirrored in several other Blue Springs schools. The beauty of a school like James Lewis is really found in the level of engagement and intellectual challenge one can observe visiting its classrooms. These are kids who thrive when thinking deeply about books and who love to share their insights with others. Their concentration when reading is almost impenetrable and their zeal to understand is palpable.

We know that the vast majority of children's time is spent reading narrative text, particularly in primary classrooms (Duke 2000), and we know that background knowledge, often gleaned from informational texts, is a critical component of comprehension (Fisher and Frey 2009). Yet in too many classrooms, we don't fully utilize rich informational texts that are inviting and engaging to children throughout the grade spectrum. This is not the case at James Lewis.

Here, teachers and students have gone beyond comprehension strategy instruction to create a flourishing center of intellectual engagement across the curriculum, and it's important to note that children are as passionately engaged in reading informational text as they are narrative. At James Lewis, informational text is a year-long genre study. Teachers read informational text aloud with great passion, and students are as likely to have informational texts in their hands for independent reading as narrative. Charts and photographs document children's inquiry projects related to nonfiction topics, and artifacts from nonfiction study adorn the classrooms. It is in one of these classrooms that I met Jacob.

These are kids who thrive when thinking deeply about books and who love to share their insights with others. Their concentration when reading is almost impenetrable and their zeal to understand is palpable.

Outcomes of Understanding in Informational Text: Indicators of Deeper Comprehension

Cognitive Outcomes for Learners

1. We **imagine ourselves in real-world situations, immersed in ideas**. We have compelling questions. We take on the role of scientist, social scientist, mathematician:
   - We begin to **understand thought leadership**—we explore and seek to understand the lives of those who have made significant contributions to a field and begin to imagine how we might do the same.
   - We **understand the problems that led to discoveries and new solutions** in the scientific, technological, or social scientific world. We have a sense of the elements that make a situation problematic and of the steps needed to solve the problem.

2. We **experience a memorable emotional response**. We may feel a passion to learn more or compassion for others who are affected by a problem.

3. We **experience the aesthetic**—we feel a sense of wonder about the complexities and nuances related to a concept we are learning. We may feel compelled to reread portions and dig more deeply into the topic.

4. We **revisit and rethink**—we reread texts or explore new ones to learn more about a concept.

5. We **generate our own hypotheses and theories** about why and how things happen in the natural and social world; we check our hypotheses against those that have been tested. We may feel moved to take action to mitigate a conflict in the world.

6. We **direct our energy to comprehending a few ideas of great import**. We develop a sense of what matters most, what is worth remembering, and have the confidence to focus on important ideas rather than on details unimportant to the larger text. We **evaluate the information** for credibility and bias.

7. We **recognize patterns and text structures**, including
   - **Cause/effect**—we use our background knowledge to discern how events affect one another.
   - **Comparisons and contrasts**—we develop a sense of how concepts are similar and different.
   - **Chronology**—we sense the general order of development or the progression of a series of ideas.
   - **Problem/solution**—when a problem is introduced, we begin to consider solutions and/or to anticipate solutions that may be presented in the text; we anticipate new problems and solutions related to earlier ones.

8. We **create schema**—we realize how newly learned concepts fit into our existing background knowledge and how we can make sense of new information in relation to what we already know. We determine whether our existing knowledge is accurate, inaccurate (and needs to be revised), or incomplete and look to a variety of sources to complete missing schema.

9. We **recognize the influence of beliefs, values, and opinions**. We may experience an affirmation of existing beliefs/values/opinions and/or sense newly developing ones related to the text and can give evidence to support them.

10. We **remember**. We develop the sense of permanence that comes with deeply understanding something; we know that we'll be able to apply concepts in new situations.

Figure 4.1

Jacob's Conference

"I really want to be an astronaut when I grow up. I know a lot about the space station." Jacob loves to read about space. He looks up from his book, *Eyewitness: Space Exploration* (DK 2004) during one of my visits to his fifth-grade classroom at James Lewis. I had just taught a lesson in which I thought aloud about how readers use relevant prior knowledge, or schema, to comprehend more deeply. I moved into conferring with students to check their application of the strategy in their independent reading. I was not terribly surprised at the rather superficial nature of Jacob's response, but I wanted to be very thoughtful about my approach in the conference. Several years ago, I might have said, "Great connection, Jacob. Mark it on a sticky note, keep going." Not anymore! I asked him to give me a moment while I considered how I wanted to respond to him. I was cognizant that I wanted to actually *teach* him something that would be valuable to him as a reader and I was determined to take my time to consider the most effective approach.

I reflected on three different directions I might take in the conference in order to help Jacob understand the concepts in his book more deeply.

In traditional nonfiction comprehension instruction (more like assessment than instruction), Jacob might have been a member of a group of students who read the same text. The teacher would ask questions, in either a large or small group conference, focused primarily on the students' short-term recall of the text content or ask the students to retell portions of it. The teacher might ask Jacob and others questions to assess their recall of one main idea and some supporting details, and chances are she would already have the "right" answers in mind. In this scenario, Jacob and his friends wouldn't have an opportunity to discuss the topic or ways in which they might learn from this reading experience in a way that would make them better readers or more knowledgeable about the topic. They wouldn't be learning to comprehend *better* or even learning more about the topic; they'd simply be assessed to determine whether they read the text and what they recalled from it shortly thereafter.

The second scenario is one in which the teacher focuses on comprehension strategy instruction. Jacob would be taught (at least it's not just assessment!) to make "text-to-self," "text-to-text" and "text-to-world" connections and his teacher would either confer with him or meet with a small group to ask children to share their connections. Jacob might share that he "wants to be an astronaut" or has "read another book about space" or "knows a lot about the space station"—text-to-self, text-to-text, and text-to-world (to solar system?) connections, respectively. He may make connections, but it's possible that none of them would help Jacob understand the topic of space more completely. Jacob doesn't necessarily learn anything about how schema is used in new reading situations or how he can add new information to his schema in order to understand the concept more completely and lastingly. If I used this tactic in the conference with Jacob, our conversation might stop after he shared any connections.

In the third scenario, children's use of strategies isn't an end in itself, but a tool to enhance understanding—to support their learning of new content. I knew that I had to push for more than Jacob's initial use of the strategy. I needed to help him articulate schema relevant to the text and discuss what he understood about the text and its content *because* of his schema. I wanted him to connect and store new information in association with what he already knew, creating a more complete picture of the topic in his long-term memory. Perhaps most important, I wanted him to use the kind of thinking he used that day in new texts and learning contexts in the future.

Responding to Jacob: Putting Scenario Three into Practice

"Okay, Jacob," I said, resuming the conference after a few moments of silence, "you're saying that you have a connection to this text because you really want to be an astronaut when you grow up and you know a lot about the space station." I always try to restate the child's response so he has a chance to hear it again and reflect on it more. "Now I have an important question to ask. Do you have additional schema that helps you understand this book?" He looked up, clearly surprised, and appeared to be thinking, "I just told you my connection, isn't it time for you to move along?"

"I just mean, Jacob, that I'm interested in other schema you have and how it may help you understand this book better." Jacob glanced back at the book and said, "That's all." It was an almost automatic response, but I didn't want to accept his response and move on. I used one of my favorite phrases to help him buy some time to think. "I know you don't have more schema, Jacob, but if you did, what would it be?"

He looked at me like he wondered if I was in any way hard of hearing, but I just smiled. This time, he turned back to study a section in the book that described astronauts' sleeping arrangements. He glanced up at me and back at the page several times. I waited and resisted the urge to bail him out with a leading question or idea. Sometimes I literally have to bite my tongue, but it's always worth the wait.

Finally, he said, "Well, I was thinking about my sleeping bag at home and how if I had it in space, it would just be floating around, and I would be floating around in it and we would bang into stuff because of no gravity. I couldn't get how come they aren't just floating around in their sleeping bags, so I had to reread this part and then I looked at these pictures and I started to get that their sleeping bags are totally different. They're made out of different material that's only for space; they're attached to the beds with big Velcro and stuff." He paused and appeared to be thinking back. "Then, I started thinking about people who figure this stuff out, like how they figure it out, how they make new stuff like a sleeping bag for space . . . "

Jacob went on at some length, and despite the prevalence of the word *stuff* in his remarks, he revealed real understanding of some of the problems scientists have had to solve to make life in space possible. I also noticed that Jacob was beginning to think beyond this book—he was thinking about scientific invention and the people whose thinking leads to solutions to real problems, a common outcome in informational text (see Figure 4.1, outcome 1).

I wasn't yet done with Jacob (poor kid!). Whether in a small group, large group, or an individual conference, I always want to *teach* students something new about themselves as readers, but in an informational text conference, I also want to ensure that they are building schema for the topic. I want to teach them to be strategic in their thinking when I'm not around and I want them to have *permanent* new understanding of the content about which they are reading.

"Jacob, I have just learned something extraordinary from you!" I exclaimed. His look said, "Who, me?"

I wanted him to use the kind of thinking he used that day in new texts and learning contexts in the future.

"I just realized that you are thinking like a scientist! You're coming up with new ideas, based on what you read and what you hypothesize about how things work in space [Figure 4.1, number 5]. You are also using your schema about conditions with gravity, like sleeping here on earth and all the new 'stuff' [see, teachers can say "stuff" too!] you're learning to imagine all the problems that scientists have to solve when they're just trying to make everyday life manageable in a weightless environment. Astronomical engineers have to think like you're thinking. But, Jacob, here's the cool part! I don't think it's just engineers who use their schema to begin to imagine solutions to problems. I think it may be all kinds of scientists and even inventors! I think you've uncovered a way of thinking that is critical to science and invention! You started to put yourself in the role of a scientist or inventor to begin to imagine solutions to complex problems. What does that make you think?"

Jacob took a long moment to think and finally said, "You mean that at first I was just thinking about the sleeping bags and how they had to be different in space, but now I am thinking about how people have to invent stuff to solve problems, not just in space?"

"Exactly, and I think you could use this way of thinking in other books!"

Jacob's schema about sleeping bags in space was leading him to broader insights. He was thinking about his thinking and starting to see how he might focus on scientific invention more generally. I was thrilled, but wanted him to be clear on what that meant for him as a reader.

"Jacob," I added, "I have a goal that I think you might want to work toward as a reader, particularly a reader of science. I know you're still reading this book and that you will be reading other informational texts soon. I wonder if you could read this book and the next books you read *from the point of view of a scientist* so that you could come to understand the kinds of problems and conditions that force scientists and inventors to create new solutions. In this book, you understood that you couldn't just have a regular old Earth sleeping bag in the space station or on the shuttle. Weightlessness was the problem that made scientists come up with a new solution. I think there must be thousands of other problems that have forced people to create amazing new solutions. Would you be willing, Jacob, to make a list in your reader's notebook about the problems that led people to find solutions in science, especially in space? I'm so interested to learn about situations that have caused scientists to create new solutions." I chose this focus for his goal by thinking about the Outcomes of Understanding—in this case, number 1.

"Yep," Jacob replied. "I could watch for that, and it makes me think that I might want to be the kind of astronaut that invents stuff!"

Stuff. Ah well, I'll take that on another time.

What Does the Conference with Jacob Tell Us?

The transformation in Jacob's thinking from "I want to be an astronaut" to his goal for future reading is not atypical at schools like James Lewis. It results from teachers who understand that a child's initial use of a comprehension strategy isn't a full indication of the depth of their thinking. I'm amazed by what a single conference can reveal about comprehension teaching and learning. As I reflected on my notes from the conference with Jacob, I realized that if we want students to understand deeply in informational text, we're going to have to consider some new principles for comprehension instruction in general.

1. We must **teach comprehension, not just assess it**. In a classic study, Dolores Durkin (1979) showed that the vast majority of what passes for "instruction" in comprehension is really assessment. In many classrooms, we ask questions to which we already know the answers and ask students to retell after they've read. While I believe that students should be able to answer questions about text and retell or summarize it in a cogent manner, it is important to understand that these are assessment processes that don't necessarily improve student's comprehension. If we want to help students become better readers, we must think aloud about our own comprehension processes, teaching students the tools they can use in new reading situations.

2. Whether working one-on-one in a conference, a small group, or the whole class, if we want students to go beyond superficial responses to deeper understanding about texts, we have to **give them time**. I modeled how a reader has to take time to think by asking Jacob to

give me a moment to consider my response to his initial connections and later waited long moments for him to return to the book and consider new ideas he wasn't aware he had when I first asked. Waiting them out, patiently restating students' first responses, and resisting the temptation to answer for them nearly always leads to more thoughtful responses that are more revealing with respect to what students really understand. It is worth the wait.

3. We must **probe beyond students' initial responses**. If I had been satisfied with Jacob's initial connections, I would have missed the very interesting thinking he shared about how there are people out there who spend their lives seeking solutions to complex problems. We need to start with the assumption that students usually have far more thinking to share, but we have to probe to find it. I didn't lead Jacob toward a particular response, but asked and trusted that he did have more to say about his schema. Given time and a teacher who wouldn't give up, he showed that he had much more to say than even he realized.

4. We must **consider the informational text outcomes of comprehension strategy use**. If we ask ourselves where comprehension strategies *lead* a reader, what new insights result from strategy use, we open whole new worlds of insight. For example, Jacob's schema, for sleeping bags of all things, led him to think much more broadly about the context for scientific discovery and the people who work toward solutions to problems in the scientific world (Figure 4.1, outcome 1). The outcomes are, I believe, a critical next step in our comprehension work. I can use the outcomes to help me decide on a goal in a conference and/or choose which ones to model explicitly in whole-class, small-group, or conference settings.

Back in Jacob's fifth-grade classroom, I pulled the children together after independent reading and writing and asked them to share what they had learned about themselves as readers that day. Several talked about the ways in which they made schematic connections in their text before Jacob finally raised his hand.

"At first all that was in my mind was a connection about astronauts' sleeping bags and my sleeping bag. But, I thought about it more and more and I got really interested in all of the stuff people have to invent for [life in] space. The sleeping bag made me think of cooking food and going to the bathroom [chortling from the group, of course, but Jacob was serious, even earnest] and getting dressed and just all the kinds of things you have to do to just be normal in space. Somebody has to work on all of that, to make it all possible so that they [the astronauts] can do their real work and not have to worry about just normal stuff. I was talking with Mrs. Keene and she said that I'm interested in problem solving—how scientists figure out the problems in space and even invent new things to solve problems. After she left, I started really liking solving problems like math problems and in science when we have to do a lab, I love figuring out the steps. I'm going to read more books on astronauts and space and other science problems and think like one of the people who solve the problems."

Jacob has come a long way from, "I want to be an astronaut." I believe that naming what he was doing—thinking like a problem solver—made it possible for him to define and describe what he understood. It gave him a particular perspective on life in space, making him more likely to retain and reapply what he learned. He also grew as a reader. He learned that there is more to using comprehension strategies than saying, "I want to be an astronaut," or "I have a sleeping bag." He learned that readers can imagine themselves in real-world situations and can pursue questions of passionate interest. Jacob now sees himself as the kind of reader who solves problems and will likely approach other informational text from that perspective.

As I left Jacob's classroom at James Lewis, I realized that teachers and students in schools like this have begun to explore the new horizons in comprehension teaching and learning in a way I never could have imagined when I first began to read about strategy instruction. They have created physical spaces conducive to in-depth thought, provocative conversation, and lasting understanding, but they have done something even more significant. Teachers here and in many schools throughout the country understand that they must create an unseen as well as a seen environment in which children are expected *and taught* to comprehend at the highest levels. Ultimately, it matters less that Jacob made a text-to-self connection than that he left the conference with a new way of thinking about books and the topics that intrigue him so much.

Weaving the Outcomes into Our Work with Students

We need to consider ways to make the Outcomes of Understanding (both narrative and informational) come alive in the classroom. In Jacob's case, I named two of the outcomes—immersing oneself in real-world problems/imagining solutions and generating a theory or hypothesis about how something works—during a conference with him. When listening to Jacob, I realized that he was exhibiting two of the outcomes without really knowing it. I had to be aware of the outcomes when Jacob used them on his own and to tell the truth, I can't remember each outcome, so I carry the list with me when I confer. Then, my job is to label a child's thinking and describe it, thus increasing the likelihood that students will use it again—in Jacob's case, I hope he'll approach other texts as a problem solver and as someone who generates theories about how things work. Conferences are a key venue for bringing the informational or narrative outcomes into the classroom, but it's also possible to be explicit about an Outcome of Understanding through a think-aloud lesson.

Mindy is an early-career second-grade teacher. She was part of a book study group that read *To Understand* and has been trying to implement some of the suggestions from the book. She too was interested in seeing if her second graders could go a bit deeper in their thinking. She decided to incorporate some of the Outcomes of Understanding into her think-alouds and tried it first with informational text. I happened to be in the classroom observing and taking notes the day Mindy tried her first think-aloud with the whole class.

Mindy used *A Bird or Two: A Story About Henri Matisse* (Le Tord 1999), a book brimming with information about the painter but told in the form of a story. She gathered the whole class before her on the floor.

"Good morning everyone! I'm so happy to see you all this morning because I have a great book that I want to share with you. You've been talking about different artists in Art and I wanted to bring one of my favorite books

*T*eachers . . . in many schools throughout the country understand that they must create an unseen as well as a seen environment in which children are expected and taught to comprehend at the highest levels.

about an artist into the classroom today. We've been talking about how readers *create images* to help them more fully understand the texts they're reading, and you've been paying attention to the images you have in your minds and your hearts as you read independently. Today I'm going to think aloud about images in this book by Bijou Le Tord called A *Bird or Two*. It's about the artist Henri Matisse, who died about the time my mother was born—in 1954. He was French and spent much of his time in the French city called Nice, which is near the Mediterranean Sea. He loved to paint by the sea and the book opens with Matisse returning to the sea in the winter. In the beginning you'll hear about how being near the water changed his paintings."

After reading several pages, Mindy stopped for her first think-aloud. "I was looking at this illustration while I read"—Mindy gave the children a close-up look at one of the whimsical illustrations drawn in the style and with some of the vivid colors Matisse favored—"and it gave me a great image in my mind. As we look out of the window toward the sapphire blue of the sea, I found that I could actually hear the waves and feel the sea breeze blowing through the palm trees. I see Matisse in the foreground here, drawing, and I can almost hear the sound his hand makes as it moves across the canvas. This picture just captures for me what it must feel like to be an artist like Matisse—totally immersed, concentrating and concerned only with the painting at that moment, like nothing else in the world matters.

"And, I love the words on this page: 'He used it [the color black] on pure white paper as a fine, simple, curving line, which he called an arabesque.' I could read those words again and again with my image of the sounds of the sea, the breeze, and Matisse's hand moving across the canvas in my mind. I have an image, but it's what the image helps me understand that I want you to remember. I have—and this is a new word that I'm going to write on our outcomes chart as I say it—I have a *sense of the aesthetic* [Figure 4.1, outcome 3]. That means that my images help me to find the real beauty in what Matisse is doing. I see the beauty in the illustration, but I also have a sense of it in my heart. To have a sense of the aesthetic means that I have a strong feeling about how beautiful this page and this moment in Matisse's life really is. It may be different for you, but for me it is very beautiful. He is sitting with his drawing pad with the sea in the background and it's almost like we're getting to spy on him in a very private moment.

He's all alone and immersed in his drawing—I find the scene very moving—it actually gives me chills. It appeals to my sense of the aesthetic. My images—hearing the sea, feeling the breeze, hearing his hand move across the canvas—helped me realize that this page is very beautiful to me; I have a sense of the aesthetic, I'm aware of that which I find beautiful. I'll be so interested to see, in the coming pages, if you have a sense of the aesthetic too. I'll be interested to see if there is a page where you have vivid images and if those images help you to discover the beauty on the page."

Mindy's masterful think-aloud showed how her use of a comprehension strategy allowed her to segue into a discussion of an outcome—in this case having a sense of the aesthetic in an informational text. She defined aesthetic, used it repeatedly in the context of her think-aloud, recorded the word and a short definition on the classes' outcomes chart, and encouraged children to discover their own sense of beauty in the coming pages of the read-aloud. She went on to ask them to first share images and then talk about whether those images led them to find anything beautiful—if they had their own sense of the aesthetic. They discussed Matisse, the techniques that make his work so recognizable, and the era in which he lived.

On a page where the words "Matisse made us 'hear' with our eyes the music he painted in his pictures" are printed alongside a vividly colored painting of a woman with a guitar, Isabel said, "I have an image. I can hear the lady playing the guitar and the guitar sounds like the green and red in the painting. It's a soft song in my head and it sounds like what you see—it's green and red in my head. I have a sense of the s'tic right there on that page." Mindy gently reminded her of the pronunciation of *aesthetic* and we exchanged a glance. These second graders were learning what most of us learn in high school or college at the same time they were learning about Matisse. They were learning to focus on what they found beautiful and compelling and they were able to articulate how an image leads to an outcome.

Whether we point out and label when a child uses an outcome on her own or whether we incorporate an outcome into a think-aloud lesson, the critical concept to remember is that when we label and describe an outcome, we dramatically increase the likelihood that children will use it in their independent reading. If, as I've suggested, outcomes are markers of deeper understanding, we're actually teaching children to understand more deeply.

Your Turn

As with narrative text, there is no better way to understand the informational Outcomes of Understanding than to experiment with them in your own reading. I've excerpted a few paragraphs from the book *Michelangelo* by Gilles Neret. As you read these paragraphs, take notes about how you come to understand. Do you use comprehension strategies? Try to pay attention to the ways your mind works when you are trying to make sense of text for the first time. Review the Outcomes of Understanding. Do you find yourself using any?

> *Michelangelo never made any mystery of the fact that his entire life, from youth to old age, was consumed by passion. He seems to have been caught up in a whirlwind, like that of Dante's Inferno, which might sweep him up to Paradise or hurl him down to Hell. In the work that emerged from this vortex, the faces of handsome adolescent boys play a prominent role. Traditionally, this fact has been passed over in silence. Indeed, there were many clumsy attempts to conceal it out of a misplaced sense of the artist's dignity. Censorious morality, unable to comprehend Michelangelo's monumental creative strength, drew a veil over these figurations of a love at once carnal and mystic.*
>
> *Yet in Michelangelo's work, passion and creation are born of the same fire. His poems themselves are, in his own words, made of "rugged, white-hot lava." The torment of this perpetual flame was such that he sometimes wished he had plucked out his eyes and thus denied himself knowledge of beauty: "If in my youth I had realized that the sustaining splendour of beauty with which I was in love would one day flood back into my heart, there to ignite a flame that would torture me without end, how gladly would I have put out the light of my eyes!"*
>
> *Now that we are no longer burdened by such hypocrisy, the edifice (the David) which Michelangelo sought to raise to his God stands revealed in all its glory—an edifice dedicated entirely to beauty. It is a triumph which has no equivalent in the history of art—a unique phenomenon, which has bred no heirs. Its success is due to the artist's ability to harness apparently conflicting forces. His mind united a feminine sensibility with a strength worthy of Hercules.*
>
> —FROM GILLES NERET, *MICHELANGELO*

Reread the piece, taking more notes about the cognitive processes you use to understand. Now ask yourself this question: In what ways do the processes I've just used help me to understand this piece better? For example, if you noticed that you visualized the David or perhaps the ceiling of the Sistine Chapel, how did those images help you understand these paragraphs more completely? Or, if your images caused you to envision the work as it was being sculpted, how did they help you understand the text better? Did you have images of Michelangelo himself? In what ways were those images different from what you had imagined before? What new information did you glean from the text? Did any of your existing background knowledge change to accommodate the new information?

Neret quotes Michelangelo himself, and I find these statements the most extraordinary and compelling (Figure 4.1, outcome 2). When he writes that "food is only what burns and scorches, and in what brings others death I must find life," I find myself rereading these quotes to get a clearer sense (outcome 4) of his fervent, feverish need to create—an all-consuming and ceaselessly demanding drive to convert stone into sculpture, canvas into paintings.

Michelangelo, *The David*

When I read, "If in my youth I had realized that the sustaining splendour of beauty with which I was in love would one day flood back into my heart, there to ignite a flame that would torture me without end, how gladly would I have put out the light of my eyes!" I experience an almost physical pain in trying to understand the artist. His sense of the aesthetic causes him to teeter between genius and madness, nearly imperiling him and all the work that came from his hands and his soul. He seems to experience beauty far more intensely than most of the rest of us who appreciate it, but are not compelled to create it with such fervor. He almost seems a slave to the aesthetic, which causes me to remember some of his unfinished sculptures of slaves in which the shapes of the bodies are only just emerging from the stone.

I didn't realize (outcome 7) the role that young men played in his work and his story, nor did I understand that there was an effort to silence that part of his story. I can hypothesize (outcome 5) that the doctrine of his religious beliefs and the mores of the era conflicted so violently with what we now believe to be his homosexuality that his torment was great. From that suffering, he shaped the images and monuments that we find so breathtaking today.

In Chapters 2 and 4, I've described patterns of thought—the Outcomes of Understanding—in narrative and informational text. It was after noticing these patterns, indicators of deeper understanding that I began to think about incorporating them into the classroom. What would happen, I wondered, if we thought aloud for children about how readers experience these outcomes—how they feel empathetic or feel compelled to reread to understand more subtle meanings, for example—wouldn't they begin to use the outcomes in their own reading as well? Wouldn't they want to be the kind of reader who experiences empathy or the desire to pause and ponder?

What I found, of course, is that children throughout the grade spectrum were fascinated and delighted to be part of that group of readers who experience empathy, a memorable emotional response, or who are able to reach more global conclusions by extrapolating from a small portion of the text. It takes so little time and effort on our part: Ask them to reflect on how using a comprehension strategy helped them understand more deeply, wait for the response, and name what outcome the child has used! You may well get responses that don't easily fit one of the outcomes given here. You and your students will want to add to my list—there isn't any single finite, "right" list. These outcomes are based in my experiences and observations in classrooms. Yours may well be different. Whatever you discover, be sure to record it in a visible way to serve as a reminder that there are pinnacles of understanding—experiences that make the text or content memorable—for all of us and that your students are able to name and describe them for themselves.

We all know the joy that young children bring to the classroom when they first arrive—they want to know everything about everything. Their natural curiosity leads them to spend extended periods of time with informational text and to ask (what seems like) thousands of questions about

What would happen, I wondered, if we thought aloud for children about how readers experience these outcomes— how they feel empathetic or feel compelled to reread to understand more subtle meanings— wouldn't they begin to use the outcomes in their own reading as well?

topics in the natural and social world. Our challenge is to help children sustain that enthusiasm into their upper elementary, middle, and high school years. We need to consider the conditions in which young children thrive as learners and replicate them through inquiry-based instructional models in the upper grades. We need to help kids like Jacob discover and pursue their passions. When they do, we can help sustain the learning by naming and describing (using the Outcomes of Understanding) experiences they have when they understand deeply. This will be enormously helpful if we want them to retain and reapply what they've learned. The key is to create classroom environments, like those at James Lewis Elementary, and lessons, like Mindy's, where they are encouraged and supported as they discover their passions in the world.

CHAPTER

5

From the Inside

*Integrating strategy instruction
and informational outcomes*

My eighty-one-year-old father remembers everything. He can recount stories
from his childhood, his university days, and even details from my childhood
that I have completely forgotten. He was trained as an engineer; I wonder if
that has something to do with his amazing memory. He remembers minute
details from trips we've taken—what kind of car we rented, the names of
restaurants we loved—as well as the dimensions of each room in the home
our family built when I was in junior high. I marvel at this ability and often
wonder why, thirty years his junior, I have never remembered details. It's true
that I don't much care about the dimensions of the family room on Frontier

Road, but there are other memories, other bits of information I desperately wish I'd held on to. I'm more likely to remember scenes, images, emotional reactions, conflicts, and content about which I have a deep interest. And there is one other factor that makes me far more likely to remember an idea—I remember if I've been forced to reexamine my beliefs, opinions, and values (Figure 5.1, outcome 9)—if I have changed my thinking. For me, changing my thinking and being aware of those changes has a lot to do with my retention of an idea.

I remember discussions with college friends in which I fervently expressed an opinion, usually about politics, when someone with stronger logic or more factual information compelled me to rethink what I believed. I declared my intent, for example, to vote for John Anderson, who ran as an Independent in the 1980 presidential election, after feeling frustrated with Carter and unenthused about Reagan. As we gathered in my apartment one evening, my friends and I discussed and debated and the more we talked, the more I realized that I would be throwing my vote away. I recall the initial sense that I had backed myself into a corner with my arguments and that it was going to take some wriggling to get out of it. Then I realized that I didn't want to get out of it; my thinking was changing and I was fascinated by the new direction. In the end, I conceded their points. I had absorbed new information that altered my knowledge and beliefs. I remember that evening vividly. I can tell you who was there, what we were drinking (!), whom they supported, and what their arguments were, but mostly I can recall the shock of realizing that I had been narrow in my viewpoint and not terribly well-informed about the issues. Instead of feeling embarrassed, though, I remember relishing the idea that my beliefs and opinions could be changed by others' arguments. I was fascinated by the influences that made me change my thinking.

My dad and I retain and reapply information in very different ways. I understand and remember in a more episodic way—I recall the scene, the story, the people involved, the aesthetic experience I have, my emotions, and any change I experience in my thinking—while my dad thinks about problems and solutions, causes and effects, new ideas and details. But all of these are Outcomes of Understanding (Figure 5.1). While I'm overgeneralizing—I do remember some details and my dad can recall the emotional impact new learning had on him—we definitely have preferences, propensities, and predispositions in our learning.

It is also true—hang on, I'm about to write something radically new here—that children remember ideas in different ways, for different purposes. (I know, tell me when all this surprising information is getting too much for you!) It also won't surprise you when I reassert what you've heard throughout your career—we have to provide ways to learn that accommodate many learning styles. In education, we've long talked about how to accommodate visual, auditory, and kinesthetic propensities among learners. I'd like to propose a slightly different way of looking at learning styles: Different learners will lean toward different outcomes as indicators of understanding and as a way of signaling to us what they're likely to remember. The more we're aware of those outcomes, first in our own learning and then in theirs, the more we'll be able to help them retain and reapply what they've learned. The more we name and discuss the outcomes that seem to be present when they do remember and discuss the ways that children express their learning, the more likely they'll be to reapply that learning in new contexts.

The tenth outcome on both the narrative and informational lists (see Chapter 1, Figure 1.2) is remembering. When we don't remember or reapply concepts we've learned, it's possible that we didn't truly understand them in the first place. Teachers frequently describe their frustration when students appear to have internalized a concept in social studies, science, or math only to find weeks later that they don't recall, much less reapply that concept in a new context. We teach it, they seem to get it, but then it doesn't stick. Could this be because we're not labeling and describing what deeper understanding—the kind that leads to recall and reapplication—looks, smells, tastes, feels, and sounds like? Could this be because we aren't helping each child to explore the conditions under which he or she remembers and reapplies most effectively? Could it be that, as proficient learners, we're less than aware of our own leanings when it comes to making text and concepts meaningful and memorable? And, if we're not fully aware of our own learning habits, it may well be difficult to think aloud for students and to model the Outcomes of Understanding that may help them remember.

In this chapter, I explore ways in which we can help children remember what they learn in informational texts and in content-area instruction. We'll peek in on a comprehension strategy lesson that integrates three of the Outcomes of Understanding for informational text (these are shaded in gray in Figure 5.1), then discuss how we might share a personal outcome and go on to think aloud about how that outcome helps us understand more deeply and lastingly.

Beginning with the Outcomes in Mind

- ▶ **STRATEGY:** Synthesis
- ▶ **OUTCOMES:** A memorable emotional response; creating new schema; recognizing the influence of values, beliefs, and opinions

In this chapter we revisit Kolmar Elementary, southwest of Chicago. I was asked to work with Dana Murphy's fifth graders, a diverse group with several English language learners. Some came from classrooms where they had been exposed to strategy instruction in a workshop model (Literacy Studio; see Appendix A on the book's website); others did not.

My goal for the lesson was to introduce **synthesis** as a strategy to deepen understanding, but I was also eager to expose the children to some fascinating and surprising information about the pre–Civil War era—some information that might well cause them to have a **memorable emotional response**, **create new schema**, and **change their thinking** about slavery, all Outcomes of Understanding in informational text and/or content-area learning. In reading about or viewing this lesson, you'll see how the strategy (synthesis) very clearly parallels the outcome—creating new schema and changing their knowledge base about slavery. Much of synthesis involves changing one's thinking as one reads and is influenced by new text. The only difference between the two is that synthesis refers (in this lesson) to changing our thinking *during* reading, while the outcome—creating new schema—refers more to the changes in long-term memory following the reading. This distinction may not be terribly important for students to know, but in this lesson, I tried to emphasize both.

The students were studying the Civil War at the time and I used the book *Hidden Witness* (Wilson 1999), which contains short essays describing what the author imagines may have been happening in a series of very

Outcomes of Understanding in Informational Text: Indicators of Deeper Comprehension

Cognitive Outcomes for Learners

1. We **imagine ourselves in real-world situations, immersed in ideas**. We have compelling questions. We take on the role of scientist, social scientist, mathematician:

   - We begin to **understand thought leadership**—we explore and seek to understand the lives of those who have made significant contributions to a field and begin to imagine how we might do the same.
   - We **understand the problems that led to discoveries and new solutions** in the scientific, technological, or social scientific world. We have a sense of the elements that make a situation problematic and of the steps needed to solve the problem.

2. We **experience a memorable emotional response**. We may feel a passion to learn more or compassion for others who are affected by a problem.

3. We **experience the aesthetic**—we feel a sense of wonder about the complexities and nuances related to a concept we are learning. We may feel compelled to reread portions and dig more deeply into the topic.

4. We **revisit and rethink**—we reread texts or explore new ones to learn more about a concept.

5. We **generate our own hypotheses and theories** about why and how things happen in the natural and social world; we check our hypotheses against those that have been tested. We may feel moved to take action to mitigate a conflict in the world.

6. We **direct our energy to comprehending a few ideas of great import**. We develop a sense of what matters most, what is worth remembering, and have the confidence to focus on important ideas rather than on details unimportant to the larger text. We **evaluate the information** for credibility and bias.

7. We **recognize patterns and text structures**, including

   - **Cause/effect**—we use our background knowledge to discern how events affect one another.
   - **Comparisons and contrasts**—we develop a sense of how concepts are similar and different.
   - **Chronology**—we sense the general order of development or the progression of a series of ideas.
   - **Problem/solution**—when a problem is introduced, we begin to consider solutions and/or to anticipate solutions that may be presented in the text; we anticipate new problems and solutions related to earlier ones.

8. We **create schema**—we realize how newly learned concepts fit into our existing background knowledge and how we can make sense of new information in relation to what we already know. We determine whether our existing knowledge is accurate, inaccurate (and needs to be revised), or incomplete and look to a variety of sources to complete missing schema.

9. We **recognize the influence of beliefs, values, and opinions**. We may experience an affirmation of existing beliefs/values/opinions and/or sense newly developing ones related to the text and can give evidence to support them.

10. We **remember**. We develop the sense of permanence that comes with deeply understanding something; we know that we'll be able to apply concepts in new situations.

Figure 5.1

early photographs called daguerreotypes. The book allowed us to look at the very personal face of slavery and challenged some of our perceptions about it. I wanted the children to become aware of the ways in which their thinking changed (part of synthesis) as we read the short essays and to discuss the ideas from the book in the large group as well as in pairs before sending them off to read independently.

In content-area lessons, the instruction related to the strategy is important, but certainly not more important than learning new content. In this lesson, I tried to balance the strategy goal with the content goal. The responses to instruction were, in my experience, very typical for an initial lesson on both the strategy and the content. There was a wide range of depth (and lack thereof) in their reactions to a challenging text, yet I think we got a glimpse of how far children can go in their thinking.

Strategies and Outcomes in Action

▶ *If you are watching the video, view **Synthesis, Segment 1**, now.*

In the beginning of the lesson, I introduced synthesis (without using the word—yet!) to these fifth graders by using the metaphor of a winding road in the woods. (For a fuller explanation of synthesis in action, see Appendix B on the book's website.) Because it was the beginning of the strategy study, I wanted to connect the concept of synthesis to an image that the children could easily create in their minds as they progressed through the unit of study. Though this school is in an urban area and there is a very real possibility that some of the children have never been on a winding road in the woods, I believe the metaphor gives them a viable image to use to remember what synthesis is. I use metaphors like this for each of the strategies when I introduce them— they are images that we can return to repeatedly as we progress through a strategy study. (See Appendix C on the book's website for a planning guide for a strategy study.)

My goal in the early part of this lesson was to spark children's fascination with the strategy through a kind of storytelling. I knew that they were more likely to retain and reapply what they've been taught about synthesis if it was introduced in a narrative context. I wanted to speak to them in a way that revealed my fascination with the life of the mind. I wanted to acknowledge that, in their earlier years in school, teachers may not have taught them directly about how thinking works but they can learn now how to manipulate their own thinking to better understand the text they read. I didn't introduce any of the Outcomes of Understanding in this early stage of the lesson; I was concerned that just dropping an outcome into the discussion might sound inauthentic or contrived. I wanted to weave them into the conversation as it evolved. I also had my hands full in terms of introducing a strategy and some very new history content! My hope was that as the lesson progressed, we would begin to uncover some outcomes in the discussion.

▶ *If you are watching the video, view **Synthesis, Segment 2**, now.*

In this segment, I introduced *Hidden Witness*. The author, Jackie Napolean Wilson, hypothesizes about the subjects of the photos—slaves and slave owners in the American South. Some of the pictures and accompanying commentary are truly surprising because they highlight slaves who had been taught to read and write and who were (minimally) a part of the plantation owners' families. Wilson notes that the subject of one such photograph was "still a slave from cradle to grave" but that she had become enough a part of the family to be pictured with the slave owner and his children. The essays accompanying the daguerreotypes are short, potent, and sophisticated pieces in which Wilson imagines what may have been happening in the photo.

At this stage in the lesson, I took a long period of time, perhaps longer than I should have, to let the children know that they were about to hear a text written for adults—one that had some words they wouldn't understand. I wanted them to know that I trusted them to understand a book that others might consider too difficult for them and wanted them to feel a part of the inner circle of readers who, because of their fascination for a topic, may tackle a challenging text. My goal was to show them not only that I believed they could understand the text (with the support of a think-aloud), but that they might experience far more memorable insights because the text was more challenging. I wanted to show them that teachers are their advocates when we choose books to read aloud and that our expectation is that the books will affect them profoundly.

I was also able to slip in a reference to one of the outcomes when I mentioned that what I thought I knew about the American Civil War, slavery, and African Americans had been challenged and changed by this book. Though I didn't explicitly label it as such, I was referring to outcome 8: adding new schema to existing background knowledge and reshaping it to accommodate the new information.

► *If you are watching the video, view **Synthesis, Segment 3**, now.*

In this segment, I introduced synthesis and seized the opportunity for a little word work along the way. I wanted them to see the unusual spelling, given the word's phonemes, and I wanted them to linger a bit as they watched me write it because I knew that the longer they looked at the word, the more likely they would remember it, especially when they tried to write it. Though phonics instruction isn't what most fifth graders need, I do find it useful to introduce sophisticated vocabulary syllable by syllable so they can hear and see the word slowly.

Some of the children had studied synthesis in fourth grade and I was delighted to hear both Chloe and John define the term. They touched upon the two distinct types of synthesis—during and after reading (see Appendix B on the book's website)—so clearly. I did miss a great opportunity in this segment, however. I was so happy to hear the children's clear definitions of synthesis that I neglected to connect back to my earlier metaphor about how synthesis is a winding road in the woods. How I wish I could have those few minutes back—it would have made the lesson so much clearer. I love the metaphor but just forgot to use it again and therefore lost the opportunity for them to reimagine their minds at work, twisting and turning and changing paths as they read. Nonetheless, a strong definition of synthesis emerged from the discussion: Synthesis is the process of changing your thinking as you read and then pulling together all that you know, think, feel, and believe (including information from other sources) when you're done reading.

Though it is not in the video, there was an interesting moment when Mason described a novel he read recently. He went on about the plot at some length (which is why this segment is on the cutting-room floor!) and I remember feeling anxious about moving on with the lesson. What, I wondered, was the point of listening to a protracted description of a book the other kids hadn't read? I decided not to interrupt him, though, hoping that I could turn his example into a teachable moment for the rest of the class. Sure enough, when I asked Mason why he had thought of that book when we were discussing synthesis, he replied, "Because when I was reading it, it kind of changed my thinking." I was able to restate his response as another definition of synthesis, which offered the other students a chance to hear the term applied to one of their peers' thinking processes.

This segment included a bit of vocabulary instruction and my first think-aloud in this lesson. I chose to introduce the word *daguerreotype* because it is used so frequently in the book and because it is fundamentally important to understanding the text. Each page has one of these early photographs, some dating to 1850, and the word is used in nearly every essay. If children are to understand this book, it's essential that they know that word. There are a number of other words in this essay with which the children may be unfamiliar, but none that recur in other essays or that are critical to understanding the book as a whole, so I chose not to introduce them. We were already working to learn synthesis in this lesson and I didn't want to include too many other new words. I'd rather teach fewer words and have the children retain and use them later than briefly define a bunch of words that they're unlikely to remember and reapply.

I also repeated how much the book had changed my thinking about the Civil War era and the role of slaves. "It forced me to change what I thought I knew," I said. I admitted to them that, as an adult, I felt I should have had the more nuanced understanding of slavery that I got from this book, but that hadn't been the case until I read it. I wanted the children to know that adults' thinking and learning evolves constantly and that continuous learning is to be savored.

Much of the meaning the children might derive from this sophisticated text would come from the daguerreotypes themselves, making my think-aloud critically important. I had to support their developing understanding of the picture and text as well as show my synthesis—how my thinking changed as I read. I also wanted to reveal that I had conflicting background knowledge—I knew about the cruelty with which slaves lived, but there was an apparent contradiction in that the slave pictured and described in the essay was apparently such a trusted member of the household that she was seated with the family in the daguerreotype. Again, without naming it explicitly, I was introducing the outcome related to revising one's schema to accommodate new information as we read. I showed them that as we learn new (credible) information, we are forced to consciously revise what we know.

During the lesson, a young man in the front row raised his hand to share, but I used a silent signal (lowering my hand to my leg) to indicate that I wanted to continue with the instruction and would get back to him as soon as possible. I worry sometimes that our instruction is interrupted and our conversations begin to follow another path right when we are in the heart of the instruction, rendering it less clear. As happy as I am when children want to share and as tempted as I am to hear their interpretations,

my first responsibility is to make sure that the instruction is clear and that I'm tying my think-aloud to the strategy and content I'm teaching.

I did think aloud using synthesis by describing how my thinking changed in the course of reading the essay, but I wish I had more strongly connected my think-aloud to the word *synthesis*. I gestured briefly at the chart paper where I wrote the word, but I could have been more precise in reminding the children that my think-alouds are a synthesis, and that in a few minutes I would expect them to use the same process in their independent reading.

I read the entire essay and at the end, pointed out that my thinking had changed three times. I repeated the sentence, "But under all circumstances, she was still a slave from cradle to grave; but her strength cannot be masked" twice and shared that the essay occasionally offered a glimmer of hope for the slave pictured and described. It referred to her strength and even said she "appeared to have ruled the roost," but in the end the reader is struck by the inescapable cruelty with which she had to live every day. In that part of the lesson, I had introduced a second outcome, though again I didn't name it explicitly. I shared outcome 2, which relates to experiencing a strong emotional response. In this case my emotions were batted back and forth by a sense of false hope that the slave was part of the family, only to be checked by the reality that "she was still a slave from cradle to grave." I emphasized that the author may have wanted me to feel perplexed.

▶ *If you are watching the video, view* **Synthesis, Segment 5***, now.*

At that moment, Edward caught my eye. He was seated in the back of the group and looked a bit perplexed himself. When I called on him, he said that he had just realized that slavery began for babies the moment that they were born. He acknowledged a change in his thinking and he shared his confusion about how a baby could be a slave. I confirmed for Edward that the change in thinking he experienced was part of synthesis, but pushed him several times to elaborate his thinking. He continued to puzzle about the idea that a baby is born into slavery, but when I prodded him, he began to wonder how slave babies were treated. I was pleased that he had at least begun to explore another question. I couldn't get him to elaborate his thinking much further, but I made a mental note that, in a conference, I would encourage him to pursue an idea more and more deeply. I restated the definition of synthesis (sure wish I'd done that earlier) and tied the word to the thinking Edward had just shared, and encouraged the other students to acknowledge that Edward's had been the first synthesis of the day.

When Edward finished, hands flew up around the classroom. I noticed Alma in the back with her hand very tentatively raised. I had actually had my eye on her throughout the lesson, wondering if she was engaged and understanding both what synthesis meant and the content of the essay I had just read. I couldn't have been more wrong—engagement looks different in different kids. She had been thinking by looking up and away, checking her thinking against others around her by watching their nonverbal signals and finally venturing public with her ideas. Though Alma initially said that her synthesis was like mine, she actually shared original thinking when she revealed that she thought that a slave in the home, taking care of children, would be treated with more respect. She actually referred to a sentence early in the essay in which the word *mammy* is used. She pronounced it "nanny," which of course was not quite right, but didn't significantly change the meaning of the word. Then, however, she realized that slaves were not treated fairly when she heard the phrase "still a slave from cradle to grave." Hers was definitely an early synthesis. She referred to two places in the text and talked about how her thinking changed between them. That's how it starts!

I actually amplify the language the children use when I'm repeating their statements (I discuss this more in Chapter 8)—I feel it's important to restate what a child has just said, using more sophisticated syntax and vocabulary. It gives them additional time to think and allows them to hear what they just said in another, more complex way.

▶ *If you are watching the video, view* **Synthesis, Segment 6**, *now.*

Before reading a new essay and thinking aloud again, I told the children that they would have an opportunity to turn and talk at the end of the essay. When thinking aloud in the second essay, I tried to emphasize how my thinking prior to reading this book was altered as I read. Synthesis clearly overlapped with other strategies, such as using schema and questioning, as well as with the outcome—changing existing schema to accommodate new information—in this part of the lesson.

I thought aloud about how my schema changed because of surprising content in the text. "The thing that really changes in my thinking comes when I read this phrase, 'an imitation of white society'. . . Here I realize that at least for some African American children, there may have been an attempt to make them seem white. That changes my thinking and it makes my belief even more firm that I don't think that anyone should be forced to imitate another culture, and it gives me questions that are going to linger in my mind for a long time."

I asked the children to turn and talk and, as they were moving, pointed out that Conner invited a girl sitting near him who had no partner to join him. I used the word *gracious* to describe his behavior—I wanted to reinforce his kindness and to underscore that this is the kind of behavior I expect in a classroom community. I wonder how many of these little acts of graciousness go unnoticed in our classrooms. I'm sure I've missed far more than I've noticed.

As I listened in on a conversation near me, Charles shared what I thought was an extraordinary insight—he noticed that the young African American child pictured in the book appears uncomfortable in his fancy garb. He went on to say that the essay indicated that the boy was comfortable, but he speculated that this may only have been true because he [the boy pictured] didn't know what was happening to him. I so wish that Charles had made that comment in the large group where I could have delved more deeply into his thinking, but unfortunately, his partner used Charles' comment as an opportunity to share a connection *he* made to the book *Remember* by Toni Morrison.

Charles' partner said, "Your synthesis kind of makes me remember about the book called *Remember*. It's kind of like *Hidden Witness* because it kind of made me think about how slavery started." Though he used language to indicate that he was going to build on Charles' statement, he actually went on to his own connection, and although it was a great text-to-text connection and helped them relate to African Americans' later struggles in the civil rights movement, it revealed a need for instruction. We need to show children how to react and respond directly to their partner's comments rather than just plowing ahead to share their own thoughts. I have a feeling that these two boys might have had a very interesting conversation about Charles' initial comments had his partner paused a moment to consider what Charles was saying and then reacted to his insight. I wonder if it would have been better to interrupt them to have that conversation right there and then or if, as I decided, it was better to wait until I could conduct a whole-group lesson focused on responding directly to your partner. I'll never get that moment back to know.

It was also interesting to note that these two boys weren't yet talking about how their thinking changed—they weren't synthesizing. I wasn't worried about that at this early stage in the synthesis study because I had just introduced the idea of synthesis to the class. Nonetheless, their conversation led Charles to reflect on Robert Coles' *The Story of Ruby Bridges*, and they were just beginning to explore the relationship between the civil rights movement and slavery when I pulled the group back together.

It was another moment that I wish I had back. I cut off the turn-and-talk discussion too early—at least for Charles and his partner. This reinforced, for me, the need to occasionally let turn-and-talks stretch a little longer, particularly when children have had experience sharing with each other and when the text is as rich and provocative as this one. Our assumptions about the need to keep the pace up, to keep things moving along, may well need to be reconsidered in situations like this. My urgency to move on to the next thing may well have extinguished a conversation that illuminated the connection between the Civil War and the civil rights movement.

After a turn-and-talk, I love to ask children to share not what they told their partner, but what their partner shared with them. Obviously this enhances listening skills, but I also notice that it gives voice to children who are more reluctant to share their ideas in the whole-group setting. On this day, however, I got quite a surprise. It was one of those moments when we have to grasp madly for the right response, fearing that we might suppress the child who is sharing, but knowing that their comment cannot stand. Of course, I've been in circumstances like this before, but never with two cameras rolling and an audience of fifteen adults.

When Conner shared a connection Pedro had made to Eve Bunting's *Cheyenne Again*, he referred to changing an Indian into a "normal" person. I cringed. The trick was to figure out a way to respond that wouldn't embarrass him in front of the whole class while pointing out that the way he characterized Indians was wrong. Interestingly, Conner and his partner understood the essay I had read—they perceived the injustice inherent in trying to transform a person to fit the mores of a society. I had to find a way to simultaneously acknowledge their insight, reinforce that their connection to the other book was constructive, *and* reframe the way he had characterized a Native American.

I tried it this way. "So, when you said 'normal person,' what you really meant was trying to change his culture . . . you weren't thinking that to be white is to be normal, but you were thinking that they were trying to change his culture, his feelings, his beliefs, his heritage." I never had the chance to talk with Conner about how my response made him feel or changed his thinking (that's the downside of being a demonstration teacher who doesn't have a chance to follow through with students), but his little nod at the end of my restatement told me that he may well have understood.

I was curious to probe the idea that led Conner to share. I asked Pedro to describe how the connection helped him understand the book better. He said, "It helped me understand because when I looked at the picture, it looked like—as if that boy was really sad and it helped me understand, to see that he was really sad because they were trying to make him someone who he wasn't." I was delighted by Pedro's response and wanted to delve into it more with him, but I was caught in the classic time conflict.

I made the decision to send the children off to read independently by saying, "Ladies and gentlemen, it's time to return to independent reading. When you go back to read today, I'd like for you to pay really close attention to how your thinking changes over time, what you're thinking at the beginning and what you think later in the book.

Especially today, if there is something that changes the way you feel and believe, things that you thought you understood that might be shaken, the values that you thought you had . . . ways in which you might be surprised or in which your thinking evolves or changes." My hope was to describe synthesis in yet another way. I actually stated it more as an outcome than a strategy, because I wanted them to realize that books can change us profoundly.

Looking Back

Now that I've reviewed the video ten thousand times (a lesson in humility for sure), I have seen several things I'd change if I were to do it again. The lesson was probably longer than it should have been, though I notice that lessons at the beginning of a strategy study do tend to be much longer than the later ones. I'm conflicted about making this lesson shorter because the children were engaged throughout that time, which *is* possible when we're discussing fascinating content in a wonderful book, and it is good to know that they can sustain intellectual attention for that long. Part of my dilemma as a demonstration teacher is that I have to take much more time at the beginning of the lesson to establish rapport with children I don't know. This adds time that other teachers, especially as they work their way into the school year, won't have to commit.

In addition, I didn't follow up on the metaphor of the winding road in the woods, and I should have referred to the word *synthesis* more as I was using it in my think-alouds. I curtailed the turn-and-talk too soon and wish I'd had an opportunity to investigate individual children's thinking more deeply.

I was generally satisfied with the children's responses on the first day of a synthesis study in a complex book. Using books like *Hidden Witness* reminds me that children are far more capable of understanding complex concepts than we credit them for. If they find the topic compelling, they are more than willing to struggle with difficult vocabulary in order to grapple with ideas that are surprising and fascinating. *Hidden Witness* acknowledges the horrors of slavery while pointing out the various roles slaves played in the lives of nineteenth-century America. The children found those enigmas intriguing and were genuinely working to resolve contradictions between their existing schema about slaves and the new information in the book.

I believe they walked away with a burgeoning understanding of synthesis, some important new ideas, and perhaps even more questions about slavery than they had when they started. The children who shared their thinking definitely exhibited another Outcome of Understanding—a memorable emotional response to the content. I should have pointed this out and emphasized that they are more likely to remember and reapply the concepts they learned if they connect emotions to the facts—another missed opportunity! But there were many more lessons on synthesis to come, many more opportunities to integrate discussion of the outcomes, and lots more to learn about the American Civil War. I hope that lesson on a beautiful April afternoon piqued the children's curiosity about the extraordinary events of the nineteenth century and left them with some cognitive tools with which to investigate their enduring questions.

When speaking with their teacher, Dana Murphy, after the lesson, we agreed that it would be interesting for her to think aloud about *Hidden Witness* again the next day and repeatedly throughout their study of the Civil War. We agreed that the dual challenge of trying to understand the ideas in the text while concentrating on synthesis was a bit overwhelming, but we wouldn't have done it any other way. Presenting challenging material and asking children to engage in sophisticated thinking about it shows them that we absolutely believe they are capable of thinking at high levels about complex ideas. This is as much an objective for the lesson as learning to synthesize and learning about slavery. We are trying, in Peter Johnston's words, to build a sense of agency simultaneously as we present important content information and a new strategy. Are they capable of managing all of those objectives? They are as long as we think aloud in a clear and precise way, revealing some of the key ideas built into the text, and as long as we give them enough time to think through their insights with peers.

There was a lot to absorb in this lesson, but the children showed tremendous engagement, real curiosity about the text, and the beginning signs of synthesizing. I wouldn't suggest that we frequently pack this much into a lesson, but I am impressed that the children sustained interest and attention as long as they did. Perhaps they're signaling us that longer lessons—just occasionally—can be intellectually stimulating and that the insights they gain are worth the extra time sitting on a hard floor.

****

What makes a concept or book memorable? Why does my father retain details of his childhood into his ninth decade? As cognitive scientists continue to explore concrete answers to these questions, I believe that we need to look inward. I have realized that I remember, among other ways, when there is some type of change in my thinking. I enjoy being surprised, caught a bit off guard, persuaded, perplexed, and transformed. I understand that when ideas stretch the boundaries of my background knowledge and force me to amend it, to adjust it with new information, I'm more likely to remember, and the ideas are more likely to have an impact on my life. I think we need to talk to kids about these insights.

In this concluding chapter of Part 1, which has been devoted to an exploration of deep understanding, I want to reiterate that we need to engage children in conversation about what makes information memorable. We need to think with them about their propensities and preferences in this regard. We need to help them articulate how their minds work when they are truly learning something—retaining the information and reapplying it later in a new context. This metacognitive awareness will serve them well during those inevitable school years and classes when their teachers aren't as focused on the life of the mind as they are on the memorization of facts. Most importantly, however, when children are aware of the way they learn and remember, they will carry those tools with them for a lifetime of learning. I've developed a tool older children (grades 3 and above) can use to note their use of the Outcomes and Dimensions of Understanding (see Appendix E, "Observation Record," on the book's website). My hope is that they will begin to take responsibility for describing their thinking while reading, not only in relation to the strategies they use, but where those strategies *lead* in deeper understanding.

Comprehension strategies are tools children can draw on to understand more deeply. Synthesis, for example, is a cognitive means to an end—understanding. But what does understanding look like? What distinguishes true understanding from fleeting recall? The Outcomes of Understanding, both narrative and expository, give us new options to help describe true understanding. Following our think-alouds, a child can realize that, for her, a memorable emotional response is often linked to deeper understanding. Another can articulate that experiencing some kind of aesthetic response can make the difference between short-term memory and a lasting idea.

The Outcomes of Understanding I've defined and described in Part 1 may not be a definitive list of the cognitive experiences a person can have when understanding deeply, but I hope they are a starting place for conversations between teachers and students—conversations that will lead students to more independent, conscious decisions about how they can understand when learning and remembering really matters.

PART 2: **WORDS THAT MATTER**

Chapters 6, 7, and 8 provide an investigation of teach-

ers' oral language patterns and an introduction to the

Talk About Understanding Principles, a set of

ways in which we can modify our oral language to

deepen children's comprehension.

CHAPTER

6

When We Talk to Children

"That makes my teeth itch!" My mother was a teacher, her mother was a teacher, her aunt was a teacher, her uncle was a teacher, and they all shared dozens of little sayings and behaviors that they brought home from the classroom. My mother and the other teachers in her family used this little gem when someone said something grammatically incorrect. For example, if I said, "Me and my friends are gonna go for a bike ride," she responded with, "When you can say that in a way that does not make my teeth itch, I'll consider your request." I heard my great aunt say it to the mailman once and was mortified! My mother said it with a mischievous sparkle in her eye, but she actually made us go back and restate the request using the grammatically correct language. "My friends and I would like to . . . " Woe to anyone who pointed out that people's teeth don't itch! She simply couldn't stand the sound of language misused. My great aunt was also a stickler for posture. She ran her fingernail down the length of my back to make me stand up straight—this continued well into my twenties. Can you imagine having these people as your teachers?

There must be something genetic about it because sure enough, in my own classroom, the first time someone said, "Me and my friends . . . ," before I could even think about it, I heard myself saying, "Honey, that makes my teeth itch. Let's try it this way: 'My friends and I . . .' Which sounds more like scholarly language?" My students protested, but before you knew it, "That makes my teeth itch" became a part of the classroom vernacular. I love the sound of language spoken masterfully and I wanted them to appreciate its beauty, too.

Examining our language with children isn't just about grammar, however. I have come to believe that the way we speak to children, the questions we ask, and the way we encourage them to interact with each other have everything to do with the depth and staying power of their comprehension, the topic of Part 1 of this book. If we ask questions like, "What do you like about that character?" we can expect to receive answers like, "He's cool." If we refer to a passage in a book as "my favorite section—I just loved it," we can expect them to say, "I liked that part." And we all know how long they're likely to remember that passage—about as long as it takes for them to text (surreptitiously) the cute girl (boy) across the room.

If, however, we say that a newspaper article "moved me to take action—I joined a community group that is restoring housing for the homeless," or if we describe how a novel "pulled me into its pages so much that it caused me to feel and think and even speak in the manner of the character for a few minutes after I put it down," we may experience different kinds of responses from students. In those statements, we articulate how reading evoked a strong emotional reaction or moved us to take action—both are Outcomes of Understanding discussed in Chapters 2 through 5. It's also true that the *way* we speak to children can have a profound impact on the depth of their response (Johnston 2004).

By making some fairly modest revisions in our language patterns, we can inspire a very different level of thinking in children. Put simply, our language about learning shapes their understanding.

Examining our language with children isn't just about grammar, however. I have come to believe that the way we speak to children, the questions we ask, and the way we encourage them to interact with each other have everything to do with the depth and staying power of their comprehension.

In Part 2, I explore ways in which we can manipulate our discourse with children in order to enhance their understanding. Others have explored ways in which we can help children develop efficacious oral language interactions (Johnston 2004; Nichols 2008), but I'd like to focus particularly on the ways we (1) initiate oral language interactions with children (this chapter) and (2) the ways in which we respond to their talk (Chapter 8). I introduce the Talk About Understanding Principles, a set of suggestions on ways to modify our oral language interactions that can make a big difference in how well children comprehend. Chapter 7, "From the Inside: Teachers' Oral Language and Children's Understanding," provides an in-depth look at a lesson that integrates the Outcomes of Understanding and the Talk About Understanding Principles.

Some Entrenched Patterns

I have had long harbored the question about how our oral language affects students' understanding and have made it a point to observe in hundreds of classrooms and review hundreds of hours of video to try to discern patterns in teachers' talk that seem to be more (or less) effective with respect to student understanding. Through those observations, I have noticed several patterns of teacher talk that may need to be reexamined. These are classic, entrenched patterns that we have carried forward from our own school experience. Fortunately, each of us tends to fall into only a few of these classic patterns, but when we do, it's a real challenge to extricate ourselves from these habits.

The verbal and nonverbal messages we choose in our interactions with children and the language we teach them to use may well be the most important commodity we exchange each day. I have observed numerous lessons in which the teacher (sometimes it's me!) might have had a much greater impact on children's understanding of a text or concept if he had modified his oral language in fairly simple ways. Sometimes we say too much and overwhelm children; sometimes we couch our key points in extraneous examples and stories; sometimes we unnecessarily simplify the words we use based on our perceptions about the children's needs; sometimes we're not sure where to go next. When we fall into these patterns, we may jeopardize the most fundamental need children have—to understand.

COMMON DISCOURSE PATTERNS

1. *Talking "around" the key points*—we're not sure exactly which points we're driving at and our language is imprecise, wandering, and circular until we finally hit upon some language that we feel captures the essence of the lesson, by which time we leave children wondering what the key idea was.

2. *"Leading the witness"*—we ask a series of questions or provide prompts that lead children to describe what *we* were thinking or hoping to hear rather that what *they* were struggling to communicate. We "fish" for responses when we review content previously taught rather than providing a succinct review of the content before moving on. We cut students off before they've had a chance to fully develop their thinking—a child is speaking and, to show our enthusiasm, agreement, or confusion, we literally interrupt them to finish the thought for them or redirect them to consider what *we* were thinking about.

3. *Introducing too many learning objectives*—we feel the pressure to introduce too much curriculum or too many ideas related to a text, leaving the children wondering what was most important for them to remember.

4. *Providing nonspecific feedback*—we tell students they've done a "great job" or say something like, "That wasn't exactly what I was going for, Janie; keep thinking" rather than specifically thinking aloud to show them how we might deal with a similar problem. This may leave them feeling good (or terrible), but with no clear idea what they did well or how to articulate that elusive idea.

5. *Accepting the students' first thoughts without probing for deeper thinking*—we thank a student for his contribution and move on, thus accepting the initial (and likely the most superficial) thing the student offers. We simply lose the chance to help the child discover how much more he had to say.

6. *Missing opportunities to introduce more sophisticated vocabulary and syntax*—sometimes we are so pleased to have a child share her thinking and so afraid that we're going to stifle further contributions that we accept statements with rudimentary vocabulary and aborted

sentence structure. We then miss the opportunity to restate, preserving the child's idea but amplifying the thought with more sophisticated vocabulary and syntax. The child never has the chance to hear her own ideas reflected back in a more complete and well-developed way.

7. *Failing to vary the tone, volume, and emotion in our speech*—we may miss opportunities to modify the ways in which we speak to children, thus failing to emphasize certain points or build toward particular key ideas. Children lose the chance to learn how to vary their own speech based on the content they're attempting to convey.

8. *Failing to vary the formality of our speech*—we may limit our oral language interactions to colloquial or less formal speech, missing the opportunity to model more formal language that they may use for different purposes and audiences.

9. *Segueing from thinking aloud or modeling to requiring students to be responsible for applying an idea*—we often think aloud or model something we want the children to think about or do and immediately expect them to be able to replicate our thinking or behavior without a transition from our modeling to their independent application. It's also often true that we haven't undertaken enough thinking aloud or modeling before asking children to assume responsibility for applying the idea in their own work.

10. *Failing to label students' descriptions of thinking so they can be used later*—students frequently "hit on" a larger concept in their responses that we could actually label, thus making the concept a part of the daily vernacular in the classroom. A student may, for example, talk about feeling what the character in a story feels, and we neglect to label that experience as feeling empathy for the character.

Talk About Understanding Principles

I once had a principal who understood that we fall into these classic patterns; he also acknowledged the power of observing ourselves in order to make important changes in our teaching. He asked that we videotape ourselves in the classroom but emphasized that it wouldn't be part of the appraisal process, which relieved some of the pressure. He even encouraged teachers to review the footage at home—with a good glass of wine at hand! He told us that he would be interested in our reactions and would be happy to discuss them with us, but there were no imperatives.

I couldn't have been more surprised when I viewed the video. I found that I spoke very quickly, often in the same tone. Though I was enthusiastic and could get the children excited about learning, there was virtually no silence—no time to think, and the entire lesson felt like I had had too much coffee. I was obviously delighted to be with the children, but I was running around, trying to get in a little bit of this, a little bit of that, and the resulting frenzy left the children overwhelmed and probably a bit confused. I didn't vary my oral language interactions with the children and I didn't focus with the intensity that would have made my teaching more clear.

More problematic—although I did give the children ample opportunity to talk to each other in pairs, I allowed too little time to do so (much as I did in the lesson in Dana Murphy's classroom in Chapter 5), and accepted whatever response they chose to share without probing more deeply. I used fairly sophisticated vocabulary, but often didn't define it as I spoke. The children were engaged, but it was more like they were watching me performing and I shared far too little responsibility with them. Quite a wake-up call—I realized that certain habits and language behaviors had become routine, and I needed to rethink them.

Rather than merely concentrating on how to break out of the less-than-useful patterns in oral language, I decided to focus on what the most successful teachers did in their interactions with children. I noticed that, in the most successful classrooms, teachers used oral language that captivated the children, and were concise and clearly focused on the key teaching intentions or objectives they were trying to emphasize. They spoke with sophisticated vocabulary and used complex sentences, but were careful to repeat explanations in a variety of ways, from different perspectives. Students who showed deeper, more lasting understanding—who exhibited Outcomes of Understanding—were in classrooms where the teacher took specific care to use nonverbal signals and speak in ways that emphasized understanding. The way we speak and respond makes a big difference.

After considering the patterns I noted earlier and the strengths I observed in many classrooms, I developed a set of guidelines I call the Talk About Understanding Principles. I knew I needed to remind myself and others what matters most in teachers' initiated and responsive oral language interactions with children. I want to introduce these principles here (Figure 6.1) and propose that we use them as guideposts to help modify and improve our discourse with children, thus improving their comprehension.

As you review the principles, make some notes about ways in which you already use them as well as goals you may have. We all fall into some of the patterns—try to become conscious of those you use that may inhibit children's understanding. You may find that you have additional goals or principles you'd like to work toward in your oral language with students. List those too and use these pages as a workbook to which you (and your colleagues, if you're reading this book in a study group) return. Appendix F, "Oral Language Reflection Tool" (available on the book's website), is a tool you can use to observe each other's classroom talk.

I discuss the first five, which relate to *our initiated language during instruction and informal exchanges with children*, below and introduce the second group of five, which relate to *our responses to children's language*, in Chapter 8. In Chapter 7, I provide narrative for video footage that reveals several of the Talk About Understanding Principles.

Initiating Talk with Children—Using the First Five Talk About Understanding Principles

1. **Vary the tone of our speech—speak in the quietest tone** appropriate for the situation. Garner children's attention by speaking more quietly, not more forcefully.

My family claims that I can be heard in the next block even when I'm speaking in a "normal" way, so this principle is a tough one for me. I tend toward effusive reactions to children and want them to pick up on my excitement about learning. This occasionally causes me to speak loudly and at a mind-numbing pace. My mother (the one whose teeth itched) told me that it is always easier to manage a large group of children by doing

Talk About Understanding Principles:
Ten Ways to Modify Language to Enhance Understanding

Initiating Talk with Children (Chapter 6)

To enhance understanding when teaching or talking informally to students, we should:

1. **Vary the tone of our speech—speak in the quietest tone** appropriate for the situation. Garner children's attention by speaking more quietly, not more forcefully.

2. **Vary the pace** of our talk depending on the context and the content.

3. **Vary the intensity and emotion** we use verbally and nonverbally to reveal which concepts and ideas are most essential for children to understand and remember.

4. **Use sophisticated vocabulary**, but define the words in the context of the discussion; use these words repeatedly.

5. **Speak with heightened civility and respect**, making clear the distinction between settings in which informal language is appropriate and serious learning situations that require more formal, academic language.

Responding to Children's Talk (Chapter 8)

To enhance understanding when we're responding to children's talk, we should:

6. **Use silence** frequently, giving students an opportunity to think about concepts; serve as a model for taking time to think.

7. **Restate and probe** children's responses during discussions, giving them a chance to reflect on what they have said and to probe ideas further.

8. **Label one child's ideas with language you want all children to use**; display the language your community uses to describe thinking and use the same language consistently when describing comprehension strategies and the Outcomes of Understanding.

9. **Use varied syntax**—vary the length of sentences, depending on the purpose and content of instruction. Expand what children are saying into more fully developed sentences without changing the central ideas they are trying to communicate.

10. **Encourage children to engage in spirited and informed discourse about ideas**; show passion, surprise, and moments of insight about ideas. Model what it means to **consider the perspectives of others in conversation** and revise one's knowledge and beliefs because of those perspectives.

Figure 6.1

the counterintuitive thing—speaking in a quiet voice. She noted that as children's voices rise, ours tend to do the same (and vice versa), and we need to lower our voice precipitously when we want to gain their attention or emphasize a point. Of course, I had to find out the hard way by ignoring her advice before I gave it a try!

Getting everyone focused at the beginning of a whole-group lesson is no easy feat, but I refuse to start until I can see everyone's eyes and have their undivided attention. I love a moment of silence before I begin to teach—I want everyone to have time to let their minds settle before we begin and to know that there is an important reason for gathering as a group. I want my language at the beginning of the lesson to reflect the gravitas of the lesson itself. Many of us launch into our lessons, whether children are sitting on the floor or around a table, without a feeling of calm and focus. In some cases, I've done demonstration teaching in schools where I waited silently for as much as five minutes just to get everyone focused at the same time.

Occasionally, as I'm waiting, I'll say something to the other students like, "I know that most of you are waiting and that you join me in hoping that we won't have to wait much longer for the other children to sit so that I can see their eyes. They know I want them to have a calm mind and a quiet heart before we begin. I trust that they will soon be ready. We're going to talk about things that are so important today, I don't want anyone to miss a second of it. I'll just wait . . . " If it takes five minutes of quietly repeating such statements, that's what I'll devote to it. It will take less time tomorrow. They will learn that I am absolutely serious about having everyone's attention before I begin. If one child (or several) is having a tough time focusing, I may say, "Honey, I'm worried about you. Is there anything I can do to help you quiet your mind and calm your heart?" rather than reprimanding the child for not focusing. I say these words in the softest tone possible, and if there has been too much rustling about for my words to have been heard, I simply repeat them, again in the quiet tone, until I have the children's attention.

In the beginning of a lesson, I try to speak in a tone barely above a whisper, which has the desired effect most of the time. It communicates how serious I am about the important topic we are discussing and it has a way of making the children lean in and attend just a bit more. As the lesson continues, I try to vary the tone of my voice a great deal and there are times—when I'm showing a lot of enthusiasm about a topic—when I speak loudly, but I always want to follow that with a hushed tone again. There is something about a tone just above a whisper that brings children in; it creates a shared intimacy and a sense that the group is doing important work together.

During a lesson, I am fully aware that there are children who learn by moving, and I'm quite careful not to confuse a bit of wiggling or looking away with inattentiveness. During the lesson, I let the wigglers wiggle and look away as long as they aren't encroaching on others. I often find that those who were either moving as I was speaking or in some other way didn't appear to be fully attentive have actually understood the lesson quite well; they just didn't have the "look" of the attentive student.

By the end of a small- or large-group lesson—that all-important moment when I'm giving the children the charge to return to their reading to apply what we've just discussed—I make certain that everyone is still and that I can see their eyes again. I wait until everyone is focused and lower the tone of my voice to indicate that they have an important responsibility in front of them—to apply, in their own reading, what we've just discussed. In the end, it's the variety in my tone—going from a near whisper to a more ebullient tone to the quiet, slower voice at the end of a lesson—that matters most.

In a conference, that precious time when we are sitting one-on-one with a child discussing her work, we need to be particularly subtle in our tone of voice. I believe we run the risk, out of the best intentions, of overwhelming some children. So many teachers, including myself, are so excited about the possibilities in a conference, or so enthusiastic about the book a child is reading, or so charged up from the lesson, we tend to barge into a conference, express our own enthusiasm, and scare the poor kid into the next world!

I've learned to slow down, approach the conference with a very quiet tone, and gradually reveal my animation about the child's work and/or the book he's reading. As the conference goes on, I try to follow the child's lead with respect to the level of animation I show. I certainly want to share my excitement about books and learning, and effervescence is part of my

I try to speak in a tone barely above a whisper, which has the desired effect most of the time. It communicates how serious I am about the important topic we are discussing and it has a way of making the children lean in and attend just a bit more.

personality and that of many teachers I know, but I want the child's level of enthusiasm to guide our discussion. I don't want to risk obfuscating what the child may reveal in a conference by overwhelming him.

In the course of the conference, I may note, for example, that a child has used one of the Outcomes of Understanding. I find that if I use a hushed tone, but infuse my words with a sense that we've just discovered something very important, the child is more likely to retain and reapply what we're discussing. I might say, for example, in a very quiet voice, "Alicia, this is extraordinary! You're describing the empathy that you felt for this character and this setting. *Empathy* is a word that describes the times when we feel in our own hearts what the character must have felt or when we feel like we're actually *in* the book, standing in the same place as the character and experiencing all around us the same setting that the character knows. Alicia, you've used empathy in your reading today and I'm very excited for you. Readers work their whole lives to feel empathy and you did it here, in this classroom, in this book, on this day!"

Conferences are the time for us to truly listen to children, and approaching them with a tone of deep respect and quiet may well lead children to reveal more of what they understand.

2. **Vary the pace** of our talk depending on the context and the content.

If my career in teaching ever falls apart, I can ensure employment for myself by doing one of those commercials where the speaker rattles out the words so quickly that he can barely be understood! I tend not only to be loud, but very speedy in my delivery, and the more excited I get the more out of control the stream of my words becomes. I know colleagues for whom the opposite is true. They speak in a very slow, methodical way, believing that the children are more likely to understand if they speak very slowly. I'd like to propose that both and neither are helpful. I think it is the *variety* of our pace that helps reveal the most important points we're making and encourages deeper understanding. I believe that we can change our pace frequently as we talk to children, revealing the critical points by slowing and perhaps emphasizing each word as if the children are being included in a very great secret.

If we use faster-paced speech (and there are times when that can be very effective), we need to be certain that we either repeat the points we make at that pace or in some way ensure that children didn't miss the point because of the speed. Our pace reveals a great deal about the actual meaning of what we're trying to say, and we should allow the context and content of our words to dictate the speed. We may want to point this out to children—they too can manipulate the pace of their speech depending on the meaning they want to convey.

When working with groups I try, in the beginning of lessons, to slow my speech as well as quiet my tone; it draws them in. As my voice grows somewhat louder in anticipation of reading a great book or introducing a new concept, I let myself speak a bit more quickly as well, building excitement or a bit of suspense. It's equally effective, after you have the children's initial attention using a quiet tone and slower speech, to introduce a concept with the enthusiasm implied by quick speech and a louder tone, then slow precipitously when you get to the key point you're trying to make. The key is variety—changing your speed to match the content you're introducing.

In a recent whole-class lesson on questioning, I garnered everyone's attention with a very quiet tone and slow, calm speech. "Sometimes I worry," I told the fifth graders, "that all the questions you asked as younger children fade away." I drew out the words fade and away. Then I very gradually sped up. "Asking questions is a key to an informed and exciting life. I want you to listen to the myriad questions in your mind, to pay attention to the things you wonder about in the natural world and the world of people; I want you to be driven by questions so compelling that you can't stop thinking about them. I want you to have a chance to explore those questions, seeking answers or even more questions . . . " By the time I reached the end of the introduction, my talk had reached a crescendo; then I paused for a long moment before I continued, slowly. "Today we begin a unit of study on the questions you ask, the things you wonder about in your books and in your life. Today changes the trend where young children are the only ones who ask a lot of questions. I want to help you restore that wonder to your life and I want you to revel in the questions your mind creates."

I tend toward the dramatic, I suppose, but I want to show how important I believe this concept is and how truly concerned I am about the precipitous decline in expressed questions among older students. I'm certainly not suggesting that all of us should vary the pace of our talk with children in the same way; merely that we should be cognizant of our speed and vary it to highlight the important content we're trying to address.

In conferences, too, we can vary the pace of our talk, though the variation may not be as dramatic as it is in group lessons. I try to accelerate my talk when I'm responding to an exciting advance the child has made in her reading, possibly a goal she has met, and to slow the pace when I'm suggesting next steps for a child. Often in a conference, it's hard to know what direction a child should take next, so when I decide upon the challenge I want to suggest for a particular child, I want to make certain that I'm concise and direct—and that I'm not speaking too quickly. I want to repeat the suggestions or goals and ask the child to restate what I've suggested as well. There is often a time at the end of the conference when I'm hoping to build enthusiasm for trying a new skill or strategy when I pick up my pace in order to emphasize that meeting that goal will be a major step forward for the child.

If, for example, I am conferring with a child who is working to apply questioning in her reading, I might check in first to identify the questions she has already asked. I would be likely to ask what those questions led to—what the child understands now about the text that she didn't understand before she asked the question. Very often, the response will be identifiable as one of the Outcomes of Understanding. In building up to discussing the outcome, I may use an accelerated pace, but when I'm actually defining the outcome, I slow way down because I'm essentially introducing new content. I'll repeat the language associated with the outcome, again at a fairly slow pace. When asking the child to think about goals she has for her reading, the pace will remain slow, the tone calm; but at the end of the conference, I may say, at a much quicker pace, "I'm so excited for you—you're going to be working on this ambitious new goal and I think you're going to find yourself understanding much more about this book!"

When we vary our pace and tone, we are also helping children to develop their own oral language variations. They, too, can learn to control the pace at which they speak, depending on the points they're trying to make. I try to be explicit with children about varying the speed of their speech to make certain points. I refer to the speed I used in underscoring various ideas and ask them to reflect on and control their own pace depending on the content they're trying to convey.

When we become cognizant of our pace, we discover that we have a great deal of muscle in terms of how we inform and emphasize points. Pace isn't something that is beyond our control, and it's a powerful tool. If children are to understand more deeply, they must be able to sort through the massive amount of speech they hear each day and to cull the essential points. Varying the pace of our speech will help make that task easier.

3. **Vary the intensity and emotion** we use verbally and nonverbally to reveal which concepts and ideas are most essential for children to understand and remember.

We can all recall working to get our emotions in check before entering the classroom. We know we need to leave our personal dilemmas and distress at the door of the school, but I now understand that emotion is a powerful variable in our teaching. In my observation, children see a rather narrow range of emotion from their teachers, and I'd like to propose that we broaden that range. I'm certainly not suggesting that we share our feelings indiscriminately in the classroom or that we lose a professional distance, but I find that children are extremely responsive when we reveal just a bit more emotion than we may be accustomed to sharing.

I sometimes begin a lesson by telling children that I'm worried about something—perhaps a trend I see in other classes I've worked with or among children their age. In the example I used early in this chapter, I told students I was worried about how older children tend to be less overtly curious than their younger peers. I may say that my heart aches when I meet a child who is less than willing to share his thinking with the class or when I hear children say that reading is boring. I believe that, within reason, children deserve to know how we feel about what goes on in the classroom and that we need to broaden our range of emotion from pleased or disappointed to joyful, thrilled, curious, jubilant, suspense-filled, surprised, elated, frustrated, outraged, worried, anxious, cautious, skeptical, fearful, or uneasy. Read-alouds are the perfect time to show a broader range of emotion and to *label* the kinds of feelings books summon in us. Children

When we become cognizant of our pace, we discover that we have a great deal of muscle in terms of how we inform and emphasize points. Pace isn't something that is beyond our control, and it's a powerful tool.

learn about appropriate expression of emotion from us, and we want them to learn to use and name a variety of different emotions and to examine their reactions for clues about how completely they understand text.

In fact, one of the Outcomes of Understanding discussed in Part 1 has to do with experiencing a powerful emotional reaction when reading. To the degree that we can describe that emotion in very specific terms and encourage children to do the same, it is more likely that they will retain and reapply what they've read.

Our expression of emotion reveals how deeply we understand the texts we share in large- and small-group instruction. We need to use carefully chosen words to express what we understand, but I believe that children read our emotions every bit as much as they listen to our words. In Part 1, when I described the Outcomes of Understanding, I pointed out that a strong emotional reaction can be an indicator of deeper understanding, particularly in narrative text. We need to monitor and share our emotions as we read aloud to show how books affect us, but we also need to take the next step—pointing out that the various emotional reactions we have are indicators of deeper understanding.

Recently, I read *Painting the Wind* by Patricia and Emily MacLachlan to a group of third graders and paused as I read to think aloud about the range of emotion the book evoked in me. I wanted my language to be very specific and to express the nuances of emotion that surface when I read this book. As the authors describe a young boy who loves to paint and waits each summer for a community of other painters to join him on his island home, I expressed awe and a bit of envy at the rich sound of the words the authors employ. They use actual paint names like Alizarin Crimson and Terracotta Scarlet Lake and Cadmium Red to evoke a scene. Any writer has to envy, just a bit, another writer who can conjure for the reader the particular smell of oil paint oozing out of the tube and the sound of a paintbrush dabbing on a canvas. I told the children I felt a bit jealous of the MacLachlans' skill with language.

The book is filled with paintings of dogs as well, and I thought aloud about how an old dog's face fills me with a sense of tenderness tinged with a bit of sorrow. It seems to me that we have too little time with our dogs. I went on to describe how the book fills me with a sense of a great silence that I imagine surrounds painters as they work. It is a peaceful book that ignites my sense of the aesthetic (one of the Outcomes of Understanding).

I asked the students to return to their desks and spend some time writing in their journals about the emotions they experienced in the book. I walked among them and reread the book. We gathered on the floor again and I asked the children to share ways in which their emotions helped them to understand the book better.

Kara read from her journal about how she actually felt the boy's longing (during the long winter months described at the beginning of the book) for the company of other painters when they came to his island home in the summer months. She told the group that the early pages of the book filled her with a similar longing. I pointed out that she was feeling empathy (one of the Outcomes of Understanding) with the boy and asked her how that sense of longing helped her to understand the book better. She paused a long moment and said that the feeling she had reminded her of waiting months for her baby sister to arrive and that her parents kept telling her that the big event was coming up soon, but it didn't feel like soon to her. I asked her again how that helped her understand the book better, and she replied that the boy waiting for the community of painters to arrive for the summer must have felt that it took forever for them to get there.

Kara made a simple schematic connection, but it was filled with a very particular kind of emotion—the longing and anticipation that children feel so acutely. We talked about those feelings and I pointed out that when experiencing those emotions, she understood the character in a way that went well beyond the literal description from the book. She captured a sense of the rhythm of the character's life—a winter of painting and waiting, then a summer filled with the companionship and guidance of other painters and a sense of community and intimacy.

I have a very different type of emotional reaction when reading a book like *Freedom on the Menu* by Carole Boston Weatherford. Told through the eyes of a young African American child during the civil rights movement, the book takes us into the stores in Greensboro, North Carolina, where brave young men and women, high school and college students, defied the law and asked to be served at lunch counters. When reading this book to children, I express a sense of outrage as the girl and her mother are consigned to stand while they drink a soda in a downtown five-and-dime store. As the story develops and the young girl's siblings participate in the sit-ins, fully aware that doing so could lead to their arrest, I try to imagine and express the younger child's sense of pride mixed with confusion and fear that her brother and sister might be in danger.

This book and others like it are not the kinds of books we use simply as read-alouds. It may feel risky to share our emotional reactions to books with complex social themes and controversial topics, but how else will we show children that events like those depicted in *Freedom on the Menu* were courageous acts undertaken in an era of egregious laws and deeply held beliefs that were absolutely wrong? I believe that it is not only important for children to learn about historical events like the lunch counter sit-ins, but for us to serve as emotional guides to those times.

I find that if I express emotions as I read books like *Freedom on the Menu*, children want to share their own. Recently during a lesson on questioning using *Freedom on the Menu*, Alexis, a fourth grader, asked in a quiet, reflective tone of voice, "Why did they have to suffer? I don't understand why the white people made them suffer." Hers, of course, was a rhetorical question, but in asking it, she gave voice to a query many have asked throughout American history. I feel proud to have been a part of the learning equation that caused her to ask that essential question. There is no answer for her question, but I believe she is a stronger person for having asked it.

Conferences provide the perfect opportunity to share and discuss your own and children's emotional reactions to books and as well as how those reactions help promote deeper understanding. Many children are more likely to share a range of emotion in a conference than in class, and we should pave the way for them to do so by sharing our own feelings about books we've read. Once again, when we read widely outside the classroom, we inform our interactions within it. When we become acutely aware of emotions we have while reading, we can share those reactions with children and they will follow suit.

Certainly the quality of texts children are reading may have a direct bearing on their emotional reactions. I'm not suggesting we avoid books that have content less likely to lead to an emotional response, but will say that a steady diet of Captain Underpants or the ilk may not lead to the kind of emotional depth we want children to experience. Finding something wildly funny is an emotion we could all stand to experience more frequently, but just as I want us to express a broader range of emotion in our interactions with children, I want them to experience a wide variety of feelings as they read and interact with other children.

In conferences, we can help them articulate emotion and discuss its effect on understanding. Rachel was a third grader who asked to read *Our Gracie Aunt* by Jacqueline Woodson after it had been read aloud in her classroom. When I stopped to confer with her, Rachel was nearing the end of the book, and I asked her to share any inferences (the comprehension strategy the class was studying at the time) she had. "I inferred that the kids wanted their mom back," was her reply. In the book, two children are taken by Social Services to an aunt's home after their mother abandons them. Rachel's reply wasn't really an inference, as the children's dismay at their situation is very clear throughout the book. I was also intrigued that she revealed little emotion, especially given the sad scenario in the book.

"Well, Rachel, I'm curious about your other thinking as you were reading this book. You were the only one in the class who actually asked to read it after the lesson this morning, and I'm wondering what else you were thinking as you read this book."

"That was really all I was thinking," she said.

"Let's just slowly turn through the pages you've read so far, and I want you to tell me if you remember any inferences as I turn the pages. Remember that an inference is something you know in your mind and heart that isn't actually shown or described in the book." I turned the pages slowly and waited for Rachel to respond.

"Right there," she said suddenly, "I was thinking something right there."

"What was it, honey?" I asked.

She put her hand down on a page where the children's aunt tucks them into bed on their first night in her home.

"I was thinking that they missed their mom."

I sighed internally because we were going in circles. I decided to think aloud to see if I could spark something.

"Rachel, I'll tell you what I was thinking on this page. When I saw the tenderness their aunt showed as she tucked them into bed, I felt so strongly

*T*he quality of texts children are reading may have a direct bearing on their emotional reactions.

that all children need someone in their lives to show them that level of love and concern, and I felt this huge sense of relief that these two children may finally be in a home where they can get that kind of love."

She paused and said, "Now I remember!" I was worried that she was going to rephrase what I had just said, but instead she said, "I was thinking that the kids don't know if their aunt is going to do the same thing to them as their mom did. They don't know if she's going to leave them, too."

"That's so fascinating, Rachel. That really is an inference because the book doesn't say that's what is going through their mind, but signals from the book plus your schema made you wonder if that's what they're thinking. What else were you thinking on that page?"

"Well, I wasn't thinking it before, but I am now." She paused to see if that sort of thing is all right! I nodded—you don't have to have thought of it before to share it now. "I can understand why the girl is kind of mean to her aunt. She's trying hard not to love her too much in case she leaves her, too."

Rachel was certainly sharing another inference, but her thinking went further. She showed real insight into the character's emotional state and picked up on a fairly subtle thread that runs through the book. The girl in the book, the elder of the two children, has clearly assumed the role of protector and has a bit of a chip on her shoulder. Rachel speculated about why that might be true and put her finger right on the emotional pulse of the character. I can't be sure if my think-aloud, where I expressed a sort of global wish for children, sparked her thinking or if it was just the time we spent dwelling on that page, but something took Rachel from "I was thinking they missed their mom" to "She's trying not to love too much." It reminded me just how important it is to have the opportunity to confer with children. I'm not sure whether Rachel would have shared that kind of insight in a group, but I am certain that all children need the opportunity to explore their emotional reactions to books with their teachers, one-on-one.

4. **Use sophisticated vocabulary**, but define the words in the context of the discussion; use these words repeatedly.

As a child, I was teased about my vocabulary—my propensity to use "big words." I can recall specific incidents when other children taunted me about my language. I can remember where I was standing on the school grounds or in the driveway of my home, what time of day it was, who was teasing me, and what they said. I even recall a teacher in junior high who teased me about a word I used in class. My brother was similarly mocked and I can recall a family meeting about it. My parents tried to emphasize that to use the words you know is not showing off and that it is fun to play with new words in new situations. Nonetheless, I vividly recall telling myself to avoid certain words in favor of speaking more like my friends. It may have been that I didn't have a good sense of audience—I didn't know when, with whom, and under what circumstances I should use particular words. But I did love language and loved learning new words. Of course, I don't want that humiliation to be a part of our students' experience, and I believe that teachers make all the difference in encouraging children to learn and use sophisticated vocabulary and to take joy in it.

In addition, I worry when I visit classrooms in which teachers seem to have made a conscious decision to scale back their use of new and challenging vocabulary. Some are afraid their students are not "developmentally ready" for exigent (I really like that one!) words; others believe that there is somehow a hierarchy in which words are learned and that to introduce and discuss "harder" words or vocabulary from an upper grade level would be putting things out of order. Still others believe that children who are learning English as their second language may not benefit from hearing and using a rich array of words in English until they have "mastered" some of the more basic words. In all cases, I heartily disagree.

Beck et al. (2002) argues for "robust" vocabulary instruction in which we define, describe, and discuss words broadly, encouraging a "life-long fascination" with words. They suggest that words derived from content-area material, but also words in which children show an interest, should be explored through discussion and children given an array of opportunities to apply new words in context. Children learn a remarkable number of words through interacting with others and discussing words—between 200 and 300 new words a month! Their capacity for learning new words seems almost limitless. Why wouldn't we take every advantage to tap into that thirst for new words and encourage children to use their vocabulary in a wide variety of written and oral contexts? I have found that when teachers share their own joy in learning new words, children become caught up in the process and discover (contrary to my experience) that using a wider range of words gives them more control over their world and allows them to communicate meaning more precisely.

In a recent lesson in Tinley Park, Illinois, near Chicago, I worked with fifth graders who were learning to infer in reading. I used the book *The Harmonica*, by Tony Johnston. Johnston has crafted a heartbreakingly beautiful book in which a young boy held in a concentration camp in Poland plays his harmonica and brings comfort to his fellow prisoners while allowing himself to relive memories of his family, now separated by the Nazis. As I thought aloud about inferences inspired by the book, I was careful to include words that, while they might be new to students, I could define and describe in the context of my inference about the book.

"I infer that, as the boy plays for the commandant of the camp, his music is reaching other prisoners in a profound way. I infer that he is able to *mesmerize* them with his music—he holds their attention, captures their hearts in a way that allows them to forget, if only for a few moments, the horror of their circumstances. When he plays, it's almost as if they aren't in a concentration camp—they are caught up in his music; they are mesmerized."

Later in the lesson, Joey shared an inference. "I think the harmonica made him happy." I wanted to capitalize on his idea, but use the opportunity to enrich his vocabulary a bit.

"Joey, let me make sure I understand your inference," I told him. "You're saying that when he plays the harmonica, even though he's imprisoned and being treated horribly, you infer that he has a moment of bliss—of happiness that transcends all of the sadness around him—the notes coming from his harmonica bring him to a state of bliss. Bliss is almost like happiness with a sense of peace in it." Joey nodded. I wanted to introduce a synonym for the ubiquitous *happy*, but I realized that this quick definition probably wasn't going to be enough to get him to use the word himself, so I went on.

"You said that he was happy when he played the harmonica, but that led me to an inference of my own, Joey. I inferred that it's more than happiness he feels—it's bliss. It's a kind of joy that makes him feel that he has escaped the confines of the concentration camp. In the middle of the most horrible conditions, he finds a kind of peaceful happiness that takes him away from it all—he finds bliss. Joey, what do you think of my inference about the boy feeling blissful?"

Predictably, Joey said, "It's good." But I wanted to make sure that he had picked up on the meaning of the word *bliss* and that he could use it himself.

"Joey, why do you think I used the word *bliss* instead of *happiness*?" I asked.

"Because it's a better word. It doesn't just mean happy, it means sort of lost in happiness."

"That's a great way to describe the word, Joey. Bliss means a kind of peaceful, reflective happiness that carries a sense of being lost in happiness with it."

Joey has a much greater chance of retaining and reapplying the word after this type of discussion. It may not be enough—children often need multiple exposures to a new word before they incorporate it into their spoken and written vocabulary—but at least we got some context, some repetition of the word, and some explanation of it woven into the interaction. It has to be better than leaving the word *happy* at the center of his inference. I also used the words *transcend* and *confines*, both of which may have been new to the children. I can't stop to define and discuss every word I use, but that doesn't mean that I shouldn't imbue my speech with words, that are largely defined in the context of my sentences.

I want to use every opportunity I can to weave new vocabulary into our conversations about books: in small groups, whole-class settings, and conferences. When I use words I believe will be new to the children, I try to pick those that have the greatest relevance to the larger context—the discussion in which we're engaged, the book we're reading, and/or the concept we're learning. The more contextualized the word I choose, the more likely students are to remember and use it. I'm also cognizant that weaving sophisticated vocabulary into my everyday conversations with individuals and groups of children makes it more likely that they'll become comfortable using such words in their own talk and writing. I want it to become the norm that we use the best of the best words at our disposal. I want to celebrate when someone reaches beyond the overused word to try a richer replacement. I never want to purposely "dumb down" my words with children. All children, no matter their proficiency with English, their age, or their present performance level, deserve to hear rich, interesting language appropriately used. There is certainly no guarantee that they will hear such language outside of the classroom, so isn't it our responsibility to use the most sophisticated words we can during our precious time with them?

5. **Speak with heightened civility and respect**, making clear the distinction between settings in which informal language is appropriate and serious learning situations that require more formal, academic language.

When I think back to the teachers I've known and respected the most, I am surprised at how different their teaching styles are in the classroom, but there is one characteristic they have in common—the respect with which they approach children. From watching Sue Kempton (2007), author of *The Literate Kindergarten*, to Debbie Miller (2002, 2008), author of *Reading with Meaning* and *Teaching with Intention*, to Cris Tovani (2000, 2004), author of *Do I Really Have to Teach Reading?* and *I Read It, but I Don't Get It*, to dozens of others across the country, I am never left in doubt about the depth of their respect for children. Every utterance exudes these teachers' belief in children to learn at high levels and their trust that children will say and do brilliant things. It's very difficult to capture in words the particular quality of their discourse with children, but there is deference present in every aspect of the classroom, from the environment surrounding the children to the way in which they lay a gentle hand on a child's shoulder.

I've tried to shape my own teaching to reflect the respect and trust I feel toward children as well. I want to let my oral interactions with children reveal gentle warmth combined with the true joy I feel in being with them as well as a way of speaking that is not unlike my tone with other adults. Children know when we condescend, and I want them to feel they can safely take intellectual risks without fear of being belittled in any way. I'm working hard in my teaching to find the insight and brilliance within children's oral and written contributions to the group, something I learned from Katherine Bomer's brilliant book *Hidden Gems* (Bomer 2010), no matter how farfetched their words and ideas may seem upon first review. I believe that there is nearly always something relevant in what children say and that it is

When I use words I believe will be new to the children, I try to pick those that have the greatest relevance to the larger context—the discussion in which we're engaged, the book we're reading, and/or the concept we're learning.

my job to find the connection they're trying to make to the discussion. I am careful to use sophisticated oral language with them, defining parenthetically words I introduce along the way. I want children to feel, in Frank Smith's words, that they are "part of the reading club," insiders, and lucky to be there; that our work together is an intellectual and joyful exploration of ideas and we cherish their contributions. I want my words to reflect the awe I really feel at the depth of their thinking and to convey my expectation that they can probe even more deeply. I want children to feel that every minute of our time together provides a chance for intellectual and emotional discovery and that the ideas we discuss are worth remembering for a lifetime.

What kind of language can accomplish all of those things? I believe that we should combine formal and informal discourse in the classroom, depending on the purpose and intent of the instruction. Hearing more formal discourse helps children to develop syntactic complexity in their own talk and writing and sets a tone that suggests the serious nature of intellectual inquiry. Informal language creates a tone of shared discovery, a kind of intimacy, and a feeling of "we're all in this together." In my observations, many of us adopt either formal or informal discourse and don't capitalize on the power of changing our language to suit our purpose.

In large-group crafting sessions (Keene 2008), I often use more formal tone and language. I tell them that the focus of our learning is important to their lives as readers and thinkers and that I expect that they will remember the content of our discussion long into the future.

I may say, when introducing a comprehension strategy or discussing an Outcome of Understanding, something like, "Ladies and gentlemen of the fourth grade. Today our work is to continue to explore ways in which our minds are capable of understanding far more about a text than the author or illustrator actually included in their words and illustrations. We've already talked about how sophisticated readers like you infer by using your background knowledge and your knowledge of the text to reveal something that the author or illustrator didn't state directly. This is a complex process requiring you to pay close attention to your metacognitive voice when it tells you that you know something in your heart or mind that wasn't actually in the book. I have today brought a book to share that challenged me to imagine more than the author and illustrator included on

I believe that there is nearly always something relevant in what children say and that it is my job to find the connection they're trying to make to the discussion.

the page. When I paused to consider all of the things that are going on, not just what's on the page, I realized that there is so much more that we can think about on our own. Later today, you'll do that too, and we'll all get to hear your thinking as you allow your mind to take you beyond the page and into the realm of the unseen and unwritten."

This introduction is certainly more formal than a typical lesson opening, but I have repeated the definition of inference three times, so much of my objective should be clear. The language is rather serious, especially at the beginning of the lesson. In addition, I'm about to think aloud to show exactly what I mean, so my goal in the introduction is to create a sense of significance about the task ahead. I want students to feel as if they are part of a team seeking to understand a complex and important concept, and that together they will notice and name subtle aspects of inferring. The formal language asks children to rise to the occasion and do the important work of great readers. It doesn't "dumb down" and make the lesson sound as if it is yet another task children are asked to do for adults. This is important to their future as thinkers, and they are about to be called upon to probe the depths of their thinking. I want to avoid the "lite" language we often use when trying to engage (almost bribe) children into learning: "This is going to be really fun, super easy, and we're going to be done by lunch!" I have no objection to fun, but I'm setting the stage for more intellectual endeavor, for deeper understanding, for work that will be internally gratifying to students when they are done. The tone can be inviting and warm, but I want them to approach the lesson with the expectation that everyone will be engaging in a discussion that will provide real insight and deeper understanding of the text. Children need to hear language used in a formal way if we expect them to learn to speak and write with more complex sentences and advanced vocabulary. Using more formal language in crafting sessions doesn't mean that the learning can't be joyful and engaging to children; it simply means that they are exposed to the kind of language they'll one day be called upon to use in more formal spoken and written situations.

It's also fascinating to watch children lead their own discussions using very civil discourse. I learned from Debbie Miller to let children lead their own discussions or sharing sessions, what I call reflecting sessions (Keene 2008). She taught first graders to share their thinking with one another in

Children need to hear language used in a formal way if we expect them to learn to speak and write with more complex sentences and advanced vocabulary.

a polite and deferential way, and I have since adapted her ideas into a strategy I call Open Forum.

Open Forum is an opportunity for the whole class of children (or a small group, but I love the whole-class variety) to share their thinking about a book, how they've grown and changed as readers or how they're applying a thinking strategy. I tell them, "Open Forum happens without a teacher and without having to raise your hands," which they love! I ask children to sit in a circle where they can see each other's faces and to engage in an actual discussion—not just sharing what they have to say, but actually building from the previous speaker's comments—around a book recently read aloud or a strategy they're learning. I place the book in the center of the circle in case anyone would like to refer to it and say something like, "In this Open Forum, I'd like for you to discuss your inferences about *Smokey Night,* by Eve Bunting. Please feel free to refer to the book at any time in your discussion. I'm not sure who will start, but when someone begins to speak, I know you'll give him or her your full attention and respond to what he or she said directly."

I teach children to share what they would like to say and then to hand off the discussion to the next speaker by calling on him in this way. "Darren, would you like to share?" Darren knows that his job is to say, "Yes, thank you, Ignacio, I would like to share." I've been amazed at the success when I tell them simply, "If two children start to speak at the same time, one of them will stop—you'll see—one of them will just pause politely until the other speaker is done and then it will be his or her turn." Somehow, believing that they will defer to each other and expressing that explicit trust in them to solve a problem, should it arise, works! Children as young as first grade can continue a discussion in this way for as long as ten minutes without needing (much) intervention from a teacher.

I've gotten children to the point where they don't even need to raise their hands to be recognized; they give a nonverbal signal like nodding their heads. Each shares a response to the previous speaker before handing the discussion off to the next child by saying, "Erin would you like to share?" I teach them to invite children from whom they haven't heard into the conversation by asking them directly: "Jennifer, would you like to share?" Jennifer can say "Yes, thank you, Grace," or "Not at this time, thank you."

Children love Open Forum and beg to have the chance to do it, but I like to reserve it for occasional use; once a week at the most. It's only one way for children to share and I want it to remain special, an event to be anticipated and treasured. Open Forum, perhaps surprisingly, engages even some of the most reluctant speakers in the class. I've never figured out exactly why this is, but it may have to do with the fact that the teacher is a (mostly) silent observer and that their peers are very likely to call upon them to share their thinking if they don't choose to do so. Somehow, the pressure is off and it's just kids engaged with kids in conversation, sort of like a great dinner party, but with twenty-five guests! You'll see an example of Open Forum on the DVD accompanying this book and read more about a first-grade Open Forum in Chapter 7.

When conferring with children, I prefer to use more informal language. I want children to feel that they are involved in an intimate conversation about their reading with someone whose sole focus at that moment is on them. I still try to use complex sentences and vocabulary one or two steps beyond the child's speaking level, but I want the tone to be casual and almost conspiratorial—c'mon, let's work on something together that you can do that causes you to reach beyond yourself as a reader.

I conferred with a fifth grader in a suburb west of Chicago recently and worked to hit this balance between a conversation among friends about a book and a call to reach further as a reader. Jacquan was reading a nonfiction book about the NFL when I stopped by. I worried because not only had I not read the book, I know precious little about the topic!

"Jacquan, I see that you're reading about the National Football League."

"Yeah."

"I wonder if you can tell me about what you've marked as most important so far." The class was in the middle of a comprehension strategy study of determining importance.

"I'm not real sure, I haven't marked anything yet," was his response.

"Okay, my friend. Here's the deal. I'm not that knowledgeable about football and I need you to be the guy who helps me understand the text under this heading, 'The Draft.' Go back and look at this page and scan

Open Forum, perhaps surprisingly, engages even some of the most reluctant speakers in the class.

it again and tell me what you think. What do you think matters most, what's most important on this page? Decide what I most need to know under this heading and then I want you to teach me what I need to know. You're the teacher."

Jacquan took his time scanning back over the section and proceeded to give quite a good summary of the draft process. I do know enough to know that he had it right!

"Okay, I think I get it," I told him, "but I want you to consider what's most important from that page. What are the key ideas you think the author wants someone like me, someone who doesn't know that much about football, to understand after reading the section on the draft?"

Jacquan thought for a moment and said, "You need to know that it's all about being fair. Guys are picked for teams based on the team's record, and they want it to be fair. They want the teams that haven't been good to get the best guys. I think it's about how they are just trying to be fair."

He actually breathed much more life into the passage than I had imagined possible when discussing the NFL draft! He needed prompting to go back and consider what was important, but he was able to do so and actually taught me about the *reason* for the draft process, not just about the process itself.

"Okay, now that you've taught me a bit about the draft, I wonder if you can tell me, Jacquan, how you decided that it was really about being fair. How did you decide what was most important?"

"I'm not sure."

"Take your time. Go back and think about your thinking. What influenced your decision about what to teach me? How did you know what I most needed to know?"

"Oh." He thought for a few minutes. "I thought you better know why they do it. All the stuff it says here is really just about one thing, making it fair so that the teams that aren't as good can get better."

"What does that tell you, Jacquan, about how readers decide what's important in nonfiction? What would you do in the next nonfiction book you read to decide what's most important?"

"I think you can't get stuck only on the words and what they say. You have to think about the stuff that's the big reason for something."

"So you're saying that if I were to read a section in a book about whales and how they get food, I would need to think about the reasons for what the author is telling me, not just about the facts themselves."

"Yeah."

"Jacquan, I wonder if you would help others in this classroom to understand that. Would you be willing to host a study group on nonfiction and determining importance? Would you work with some other kids and their nonfiction books and try to help each other decide what's important?"

Jacquan indicated that he would and later used the section in his book about the NFL to demonstrate how a reader looks for the underlying reasons behind a section in nonfiction. He worked with four students and I believe they walked away knowing far more about determining importance in nonfiction.

He was on top of the world as he led that group. He went from having no ideas marked in his text to being able to teach others how to search below the surface for the reasons authors share content in books. I needed to be clear that I was in the role of the learner and he was the teacher. He loved being the teacher and I can't imagine a better outcome for the conference.

Jacquan was on top of the world as he led that group. He went from having no ideas marked in his text to being able to teach others how to search below the surface for the reasons authors share content in books.

****

In many ways, the Talk About Understanding Principles may seem commonsense, self-evident. Of course we would use a quieter approach to engage children, and naturally there are times when our language is more formal and others when it's more casual, times where we wear emotion on our sleeves and times when we're more circumspect. We do vary our tone and pace in speaking to meet children's needs, right? I certainly would have thought that I was attentive to these basic principles when teaching until I had the chance to actually watch myself on video. I was approaching children in the way I had been approached as a child. In some cases, I was veering frighteningly close to talking down to them. I had to have a heart-to-heart with myself and honestly confront the patterns I'd developed in my oral language with children. I have to say that, these many years later, I'm still working on these commonsense principles in my teaching.

Our discourse with children is infused with subtle messages, and the ways in which we interact with children have everything to do with what they ultimately understand. We can actually *affect* what children understand by manipulating our own oral language patterns. We can help them probe ideas more deeply and retain and reapply more of what they learn by purposefully incorporating these principles into our daily interactions with children. Just as we ask children to be more conscious of their thinking during reading, we need to become more conscious of our language while we're teaching. In the final analysis, we teach to enhance understanding. If, by making a few changes in the way we approach children, we can further that cause, why wouldn't we?

We can help them probe ideas more deeply and retain and reapply more of what they learn by purposefully incorporating these principles into our daily interactions with children.

7

From the Inside

Teachers' oral language and children's understanding

I can always find ways to procrastinate when I should be writing. When finishing *Mosaic of Thought*, I redid a bathroom; when writing *To Understand*, I refinished the teak furniture on the back patio. This week I had dentist and eye doctor appointments and went to the Department of Motor Vehicles to renew my driver's license, though I'm pretty sure I could have done it online. These are acts undertaken only by the most desperate procrastinators! My husband came into my office later in the week and noticed that, while I was supposed to be writing, I was trolling around the Internet instead. I responded by telling him that I was multitasking—something, by the way, that he is incapable of doing, due to his gender! He immediately corrected me and told me of several recent studies that show that men and women are equally adept at multitasking, and that multitaskers are in fact less efficient than people who concentrate on one thing at a time and grind through to completion. Was he really telling me that I wasn't writing *while* I was wandering aimlessly in cyberspace? The nerve.

I will continue to believe, despite evidence to the contrary, that women, especially teachers, are pros at multitasking. When we begin a lesson, we may have one objective in mind for the children, but dozens of goals for ourselves. We want to merge all that we have learned about great pedagogy into that one ten-minute lesson; we want to engage, incite curiosity, manage, model, inspire, provoke, explain, and release responsibility—all in a very short period of time. That's the ultimate in multitasking! To make it more challenging, we have to repeat that process many times a day with equal enthusiasm and skill.

In the focus lesson for this chapter, I invited first graders, again at Kolmar Elementary near Chicago, to begin their journey into questioning. The ultimate goal toward which we began working that day was for children to experience deep and lasting understanding of Cynthia Rylant's book *An Angel for Solomon Singer* and be able to use questions to understand more deeply in their own books. My teaching tactic was to think aloud to reveal how I use questions to leverage deeper understanding when I read. Later, I wanted to introduce Open Forum, a technique to help children reflect and build a class-wide conversation that I discussed in Chapter 6. *And* I was thinking about what I wanted to do as a teacher. Specifically, I reminded myself to highlight any Outcomes of Understanding if and when they arose in the conversation and to concentrate on employing the Talk About Understanding Principles (see Figure 7.1) introduced in Chapter 6—and I had never met the children! There's some multitasking for you! Imagine how much more effective you can be in similar situations when you actually know the kids!

First-grade teacher Erin Lia had prepared her children for our arrival. She talked to her class about the large cameras, sound equipment, and long cables that would be snaking throughout the room. She told them about the imminent descent of half a dozen new people, some

Talk About Understanding Principles:
Ten Ways to Modify Language to Enhance Understanding

Initiating Talk with Children (Chapter 6)

To enhance understanding when teaching or talking informally to students, we should:

1. **Vary the tone of our speech—speak in the quietest tone** appropriate for the situation. Garner children's attention by speaking more quietly, not more forcefully.

2. **Vary the pace** of our talk depending on the context and the content.

3. **Vary the intensity and emotion** we use verbally and nonverbally to reveal which concepts and ideas are most essential for children to understand and remember.

4. **Use sophisticated vocabulary**, but define the words in the context of the discussion; use these words repeatedly.

5. **Speak with heightened civility and respect**, making clear the distinction between settings in which informal language is appropriate and serious learning situations that require more formal, academic language.

Responding to Children's Talk (Chapter 8)

To enhance understanding when we're responding to children's talk, we should:

6. **Use silence** frequently, giving students an opportunity to think about concepts; serve as a model for taking time to think.

7. **Restate and probe** children's responses during discussions, giving them a chance to reflect on what they have said and to probe ideas further.

8. **Label one child's ideas with language you want all children to use**; display the language your community uses to describe thinking and use the same language consistently when describing comprehension strategies and the Outcomes of Understanding.

9. **Use varied syntax**—vary the length of sentences, depending on the purpose and content of instruction. Expand what children are saying into more fully developed sentences without changing the central ideas they are trying to communicate.

10. **Encourage children to engage in spirited and informed discourse about ideas**; show passion, surprise, and moments of insight about ideas. Model what it means to **consider the perspectives of others in conversation** and revise one's knowledge and beliefs because of those perspectives.

Figure 7.1

of whom would be sticking a microphone in their faces and a teacher named Ellin Keene with whom they had never worked. Erin had been planning for days—permission slips had been returned, nametags secured. On the day of the filming many girls wore their best dresses, and one boy even had on a suit and tie! She told them that Mrs. Keene, one of her friends, would be teaching them while some of her friends filmed their work.

On the morning of the lesson, I arrived at Kolmar (the same school described in Chapters 3 and 5) early and made my way to Erin's classroom to see how everyone was faring. I poked my head into the room and a tiny boy in a freshly pressed shirt couldn't help himself and burst out, "Miss Lia, Helen Keller's here!" Ellin Keene/Helen Keller? These kids were sure to be disappointed! Though no one half as brilliant or well known as Helen Keller entered the classroom that day, we pressed forward.

Beginning with the Outcomes in Mind

▶ **STRATEGY:** Questioning (generative questions)

▶ **OUTCOMES:** We may feel an urge to take action to solve a problem or support an issue in our community

▶ **TALK ABOUT UNDERSTANDING PRINCIPLES:** Vary the tone of speech, vary the pace, vary the intensity and emotion; speak with heightened civility and respect

As is true of the footage you viewed for Chapter 5, I wanted the introduction to this strategy to be presented as a story rather than a didactic introduction to a new skill. I hoped the students would be able to imagine themselves in this narrative and begin to feel part of an intellectual community—a group of children who can go beyond the confines of literal text by asking questions. I began by talking about a time long, long ago, at the beginning of first grade, when they "were little." Their faces acknowledged how long ago that had been. We were talking about their ancient history, a time when they were little (a few months earlier)—you've just got to love first grade! I wanted to remind them of the times when, like most first graders, they burst through the door of the classroom filled with questions for the first adult they saw. I wanted them to think about the urgency they feel when they have a question to ask and are dying to have it answered. I wanted to reveal my own awe of the potential for questions to take us deeply inside the text, and I wanted them to place themselves in the story we were creating as a person who wonders.

Miss Lia (now Mrs. Johnson) has a wonderful classroom lined with books and a cozy place set aside for children to gather for crafting sessions. When the time came for the filming, I happily ensconced myself in her rocking chair and launched the lesson in the quietest tone I could manage and still be heard.

▶ *If you are watching the video, view **Questioning, Segment 1**, now.*

In the early phase of this crafting session, I began to discuss the importance of questioning and consciously tried to vary my tone of voice and pace of speech, showing emotion for how important questions are for readers. I was trying to speak in an almost reverent tone about questioning—a principle I discussed in Chapter 6 as speaking with the greatest civility and respect. I tried to emphasize that asking questions is something they're very privileged to do. As I wrote the letter *q* on chart paper, they knew immediately that I was going to write the word *questions*, but I asked them to wait, to say the word with "special care." Of course they said it anyway, but I noticed a real difference in their tone between the first recognition of the word when they shouted out "Questions!" and when they pronounced the word following my modeling of it. They drew the word out slowly, speaking almost in a whisper the second time. I told them that they said it "the way scholars say it" the second time. It may be a small thing, but I wanted them to internalize that they were beginning an ambitious new study of a reading strategy and that it was important to take it seriously.

I went on to tell them that "in any questions there are mysteries, things to be solved and figured out . . . some questions you can wonder about for your whole long life and other questions you can answer pretty quickly." I stated my preference for the former and mentioned that sometimes my questions lead me to want to do something to solve a problem or take on an issue in the world (outcome 8 in Figure 2.1). If these were my own students, this outcome is a concept I would return to again and again in our discussions, and I would encourage them to think about the questions they have that make them want to make the world a better place to live.

My first missed opportunity, a moment I later regretted, came right at the beginning of the lesson. I mentioned that I wanted the children to listen to the voice inside their head that talks to them while they read. They immediately asked me if I was referring to their conscience, and I told them that there is actually a different word that describes what I was talking about. Of course, I was referring to metacognition—to think about one's thinking, to be aware of one's own thought processes. I wish I hadn't mentioned that I might teach them the word, because I didn't follow up on it later. This is not to say that I wouldn't teach the term *metacognition* to first graders—I would and often have. I regret it because I had already built the lead-in to the lesson focused on questioning; I was ready to introduce the book and didn't want to go into a lengthy description of a substantial new vocabulary word. It would have been better not to mention it at all and to introduce it at another time.

When I introduced the book, I told them that "in this book there are more things that I wonder about than things I'm sure about . . . there are some things in the pictures and the words that will make you wonder and question, and even tonight at home, you're still going to be thinking about them, and you're still going to be asking questions of each other, maybe even on Friday!" At that moment, a voice from the crowd said, "Maybe even next summer!" You've just gotta love first graders. I went on. "This is a book that fills our minds with questions, those kinds of questions that are not always easy to answer."

In the early stage of the lesson, there was some of the inevitable repositioning of bodies, a declaration that someone "made a *really* bad smell" (that segment of the video lies on the cutting-room floor), and attempts by several children to move an adjacent child out of his or her space by brute force. I responded by simply lowering my head. I had previously told the children that I lower my head if I can't see someone's eyes or if I hear someone's voice at an inappropriate time. This little silent signal has an almost magical effect—when you stop in the middle of a sentence and look down, the children almost always look toward you and stop chatting with each other. I much prefer using a silent signal to saying, "Shhh" or "I'll wait until everyone is listening" or "Jack, could you please stop talking to Gabe."

I told them that this is a book that asks us as readers to "have a quiet heart and a still mind." I waited. Again, it's a matter of civility and respect.

▶ *If you are watching the video, view **Questioning, Segment 2**, now.*

 I began to read and think aloud about my own questions in *An Angel for Solomon Singer.* This is a stunning book about a man named Solomon Singer, living in a hotel that is very much like a homeless shelter, in New York City. The book reveals how the man longs for the Midwestern landscapes of his childhood and how lonely he is as he wanders the streets of the city. He meets a waiter in the Westway Café who welcomes him warmly and gives him

hope. The waiter's name is Angel and the reader is left to infer what that name may mean for the central character.

I concentrated on thinking aloud about questions that went beyond the literal meaning of the text. My first question was, "I wonder why, when I read this book, I have such a sense of sadness. I wonder why I feel . . . like maybe the sadness in his heart is going to last a long time. I wonder why, when I look at the drawing of Solomon Singer, he looks like people I've seen before. I wonder who he reminds me of? I wonder if he reminds me of people I have seen in the street at night."

I didn't just pose a single question and return to reading the book. I wanted the children to hear a cascade of questions, one of which might resonate with their own thinking about the book. I also wanted them to understand that one question often leads to another (generative questions), and that when they begin to apply the strategy in their own reading, they can ask generative questions as well.

Though I'm sure there were details they may have missed on this first reading of the book, I knew that Erin would reread the book several times, and I preferred to have children notice those details themselves on subsequent readings. My goal, at this crucial think-aloud stage of the lesson, was to ask questions that related to the larger themes and key ideas in the text. I knew that if I initiated the study of questioning with lower-level, detail-oriented questions, those would be exactly the kinds of questions they were likely to share. However, if I began by thinking aloud about higher-level questions, the children were more likely to follow suit.

When I noticed in their eyes that children were beginning to have their own questions, I called on Wendy, whom I had been watching as I read aloud. She seemed riveted by the book but, I guessed, probably wouldn't have volunteered to ask a question. In fact, she had made quite an effort to appear invisible within the group from the beginning. I had a sense, which Erin confirmed for me later, that Wendy was not prone to sharing her thinking in the large group; in fact she was working to learn English while managing all of the other challenges that go with being a first grader. I wanted her to know that I believed that she could have insightful questions and that, though she might not express them now, I knew that she would later. I'm not sure how much of my language she understood, but I am sure that she picked up on my tone, which was meant to reveal how much I believed that she could be a part of the conversation. Wendy merely shook her head when I asked if she wanted to share a question, but I wanted the group to see Wendy in perhaps a new way. I said, "You should see Wendy's face when she thinks. She looks like a scholar . . . The questions in her mind, when she decides to share them, will be really beautiful questions."

▶ *If you are watching the video, view **Questioning, Segment 3**, now.*

I paused again when I felt that I'd read far enough and the character and plot were sufficiently developed for the children to ask relevant and insightful questions. I noticed that particular children (whose hands *didn't* happen to be raised) appeared to have questions. Sometimes, I'm able to pick up on nonverbal signals other than raised hands that allow me to deduce that children are thinking about the text enough to have a question. Other times, as in this lesson, I was just hoping to engage a child in thinking about the book at all, and I would rather do it by presupposing that they *do* have a question than by assuming they don't, simply because they haven't raised their hands.

Hands were waving all over the room, but I noticed Canyon, who looked like he had something to say. Sure enough, he said, "I was wonder if he is actually going to get the stuff that he's saying out loud." In the book, when Solomon Singer visits the Westway Café, he orders from the menu out loud, but silently adds a wish for things like a balcony that would make him feel more at home in the city. Canyon's question had real relevance to the plot. I tried to restate it by "expanding" his statement. When expanding, I try to retain the student's meaning, but to stretch the length and complexity of the sentence to include more sophisticated vocabulary than he actually used—both are Talk About Understanding Principles that we'll explore more in Chapter 8. In retrospect, it might have been better to stick with Canyon a bit longer—to probe to see whether we could uncover other questions, but I was feeling the pressure of all those raised hands and had some sense of needing to be "fair" to everyone. In the end, though, fair may mean it's better to focus on one child, helping him discover how deep his thinking really can run, rather than flitting on to the next child and then another, with no opportunity to probe more deeply with any of them.

I moved on to Gina, whose question went right to the heart of the book, an unwritten premise—that Angel, the waiter in the Westway Cafe, may be an angel. Gina's question led to Douglas, who was nearly jumping out of his skin with a question. I made the decision to interrupt him to teach the concept of *generative questions,* the idea that one question leads to another. Obviously an introduction to this concept isn't going to be enough for them to truly understand the concept of "generative," but I wanted to pave the way for Erin, their teacher, to follow up on this idea later. I loved the children's reaction to being taught a "really long word." This is what makes context-embedded vocabulary so much fun to teach. Children love words and relish getting to learn words that are more "grown up."

When poor Douglas, who had to hold his idea for a long time, finally got to share his question, he struggled a bit, trying to pose a question about whether the waiter was really an angel. I tried to coach him by teaching him to begin with, "I wonder . . . ," but then I interrupted him. Sure enough, right there on the video, I'm interrupting a child, not allowing him to get the question out before I teach. Remember those wicked oral language patterns I described in Chapter 6? I fell right into number two!

Fortunately he recovered, and there was a lovely moment when he looked toward heaven to try to articulate his thinking. Gina, sitting right next to him, burst out and asked him if he meant "an angel on earth." He nodded enthusiastically and said, "Yeah!"

I asked if Douglas' question was generative for anyone else. Katie and Joseph asked questions. Joseph said, "I wonder if when he was a boy, he growed up in the west." I restated his question, correcting the syntax, and probed to see if he had more questions. I wanted to show children how one question leads to another and another in their own minds—also a form of generative questioning. Joseph asked a couple more literal questions and, as I probed, twice said that he didn't have any more questions. I tried to push him to think more deeply and, as is often the case, his initial questions that were more literally tied to the book led to a question that was not explicitly stated and went to the character's emotions. He asked, "I wonder if maybe he missed it [the Midwest where he grew up]." I believe that this is the ultimate payoff for sticking with a child to see how deeply he can think. I took that moment to distinguish between questions that come from the mind and those that come from the heart.

▶ *If you are watching the video, view **Questioning, Segment 4**, now.*

I read to the end of the book and asked the children to turn and talk about the text. When I pulled them back together, I asked them to share, not what they had said in the turn-and-talk, but rather to share a question their partner had asked. Raydell actually shared what *he* had asked, but his partner Kahlil quickly corrected him. "That's what Raydell said," he announced. Regardless of who asked it, the question had little to do with the significance of the story. Raydell wondered if the character drank coffee at the restaurant. I decided to push it further and was able to get Raydell to pose another question. "Did no one love him?" Yes! It was a question that went straight to the theme of the book. He went on to identify that his was a question of the heart.

The interchange reminded me of how critical it is to move beyond a child's initial response and to probe more deeply. Raydell was able to pose a very insightful question that I would have missed if I had accepted his initial question and moved on to another child. The extra time it takes to ask again and probe a bit more deeply is almost always worth it.

I decided to stick with this pair and asked Kahlil if Raydell's question made him think of a question. "Nope," was the immediate response. I was faced with a dilemma. It would have been easier to move on to any one of the other children who did want to share their partner's questions, but I told myself to stick it out with Kahlil.

There were long pauses. I repeatedly asked Kahlil to think about the questions he had, and I had to remind myself to be comfortable with the silence, one of the Talk About Understanding Principles. Fortunately, I didn't give in to the urge to move on to another child. I turned the pages of the book, hoping to trigger something for him, and when he repeated that he didn't have a question, I said again, "I know you don't have a question, but if you did, what would you wonder?" I reinforced how smart he was to take his time to think, and finally he asked if "every time he go to the place, he asked for something and it popped up." At first glance, the question may not seem terribly thoughtful, but Kahlil did uncover the fact that the central character longs for things he cannot have in his hotel—a balcony, a purple wall, a cat. He wondered, given the discussion about Angel being a "real angel," if the things he longs for just "pop up." I was delighted at that point to get a question from Kahlil at all and upon further scrutiny, I realized that it was a relevant question. Most importantly, though, the look on his face when he succeeded in posing a question was worth the world. It was a triumph and Kahlil knew it.

At the end of the lesson, I asked the children to use what they had learned about questions to understand more in their own books. I asked them to nod their heads if they understood what they were to do. In retrospect, it would have been better to actually ask them to turn and tell a partner what they were being asked to do rather than just asking for a nod of the head. They would have had a chance to state what they were being asked to do and hear confirmation from another child. I used another silent signal to send the children to independent reading, and off they went to ask questions in their own texts.

Strategies and Outcomes in Action

▶ *If you are watching the video, view **Conference with Samantha** now.*

When the children were happily ensconced in their reading, Erin and I conferred with Samantha because Erin indicated that she was concerned about her comprehension. Samantha didn't typically share in small- and large-group instructional settings, and Erin was having difficulty knowing exactly where Samantha was in her comprehension. Samantha was reading *Go Dog Go* but I quickly moved

her away from it and into a discussion about *An Angel for Solomon Singer* because the focus of the conference was to be on Samantha's comprehension, and I believed we were more likely to hear her questions about the book I had read aloud. I'm sure that *Go Dog Go* was an appropriate text for her word identification and fluency practice, but I wanted to focus on questioning.

I had not heard from Samantha during the large-group lesson—she was seated in the very back of the group and I had been worried about her level of engagement—but when I asked her if she had questions, she immediately asked, "Will he move back where he lived?" After restating and hearing that she had forgotten her other questions, I decided to probe a bit more deeply. She paused for a moment and then said, "I wonder if he feels like home at the restaurant."

I asked Samantha how her question helped her understand the book better, which was a tactical error. I hadn't yet thought aloud about how a question can help a reader understand a book more thoroughly, so it wasn't fair to ask her to try to do so. I wanted her to see the connections between her questions and understanding the book better. I needed to think aloud for her (and for the whole class) about how questions help us understand. Generally speaking, questions help us understand better by slowing us down, causing us to focus on salient portions of the text more deeply; by helping us to clarify ideas and details about which we're unsure; and by helping us to look at the text from another perspective. Questions may well lead to more lasting insights. After several think-alouds focused on how questions help us understand, Erin will want to check back with Samantha to see if she is beginning to generate more questions and speculate about how questions help her understand.

Nonetheless, Samantha had a great response. She said, "Because I didn't get that part," which showed me that she did understand that questions help a reader clarify when they don't understand something. If I were the teacher (lucky Erin), I would begin to think aloud about how questions help us understand more deeply and incorporate this notion into as many conferences as possible. Once a child has shown that she can, for example, generate questions (or use any of the other strategies), it's critical for her to be able to describe how those questions help her understand more effectively. Samantha was off to a good start!

▶ *If you are watching the video, view **Conference with Omar** now.*

Erin and I had an opportunity to confer with Omar, who was reading the book *Amazing Animals* by Drew David. When I asked if he had any questions about his book, he gave us an answer to which I'm sure any teacher can relate. "Not really," he said. Now there's a great way to shut down a conversation! I knew he was wishing that we, and

all the camera equipment, would just go away. Rather than complying with his unstated wishes, I assumed the positive and asked him to turn to a page where he did have a question. He turned the page and made a couple of statements—facts straight from the book. I asked if he wondered about anything. "Nope."

"Okay," I thought, "this is going well."

Finally he asked, "I wonder if they can catch a shark. Can an octopus eat a shark?"

It took me several minutes to figure out the direction I wanted to take in the conference and you see my hesitancy in the video. I wanted Omar to walk away knowing something new about asking questions and at the same time realized that he was very interested in the content of this book. Yet each two-page layout was dedicated to a new animal, which necessarily limits the amount of information the reader will get on any one of the animals. I realized that Omar might well have questions like "can an octopus eat a shark" but would find, because of the book's structure, that his questions weren't answered. I decided to focus on that structure. I wanted him to understand that some books may present only a few facts before moving on to a different topic, making it unlikely that he'll find answers to all his questions. Through the conversation, Omar realized that to answer some questions, he would have to "find another book in the library." He began to see that a reader's questions can lead him into research.

I couldn't pass up the opportunity to ask him to look at the book from a writer's point of view. He might, I suggested, want to write a book that is structured in a similar way. "You could get other kids in this room asking a whole bunch of questions, and then what would they have to do if they wanted to answer their questions?"

Omar was right with me. "They'd have to go to the library to get another book!"

"That's one way to be a writer. It's not the only way to be a writer, but . . . it may be, Omar, that's the way you'll choose to write your next book."

In many conferences, I try to introduce a concept—in this case, purposely writing to inspire questions—that I can then ask the child to introduce to the whole group in sharing or reflecting time. I have noticed that when a child introduces a new concept, the likelihood that children will try the new concept in their independent work is high. In this case, asking Omar to share his insights about how books are designed to provoke questions for their readers is also great for the "teacher," Omar. He will have to synthesize his thoughts, show mentor texts, and make suggestions to the other readers and writers in the room if they're going to learn what he has to teach. This kind of sharing is focused on helping other children to learn a new idea that will be relevant to them. It's about kids teaching other kids.

▶ *If you are watching the video, view **Open Forum** now.*

Open Forum is another of my favorite ways to have kids teach kids. As I wrote in Chap-

ter 6, Open Forum is an opportunity for children to share and extend their understanding of a book and, eventually, to teach other children something they have learned or accomplished as readers. Ultimately, my goal for Open Forum is for the children to have a true conversation about books and to build upon one another's insights without having to raise their hands or needing facilitation from the teacher (who is always nearby). In time, Open Forum becomes a much-anticipated time that children take over and make their own.

For their first Open Forum, my goal was for the first graders to learn to hand off the sharing from one child to another without raising their hands. I also hoped to bring the key idea—asking questions—full circle from the crafting session (large-group instruction) through composing (independent reading) to reflection (sharing). I wanted them to become accustomed to a more formal type of language—

what I refer to as scholars speaking to scholars—which I use only in particular instructional settings. "Canyon, would you like to share?" "Yes, thank you, Katie."

The children were seated in a large circle so that everyone could see each other, with *An Angel for Solomon Singer* in the middle. I sat nearby. I started by saying, "Open Forum means that it's time for the kids to talk about their thinking about a book—no teachers, and you don't even have to raise your hands." Cheers rang out. "However," I continued, very quietly, "there are some things you have to think about. This is a time when scholars speak to other scholars. This is a time when you talk about your thinking, your questions, about this book and it is a very important time if you're going to learn from others about the book."

Gina began. "When I was in the library, I saw the same book and I saw this rainbow." She pointed to a rainbow in one of the illustrations. "I think the rainbow was a sign of hope or a sign of him." I asked her, from the sidelines, what that made her wonder.

"I think it made me wonder that if he saw that, he might have known if that waiter was an angel." She asked, "Would anyone else like to share?" Open Forum was under way.

Because it was their first try, the children still needed quite a bit of facilitation. I encouraged them to restate their observations as questions or "I wonder" statements. My objective was for them to share questions they had about *An Angel for Solomon Singer*, but I noticed that they were very eager to share other details from the text and its rich illustrations. I may have overemphasized questioning in this first Open Forum.

Perhaps I should have just let them share whatever struck them from the book and let them get used to this new form of sharing. That said, I did want them to see the connection between the reflecting time and the crafting session in which I had introduced questioning for the first time. This is likely to be an argument I'll have with myself for some time!

When it was Cody's turn to share, he took the book, turned the pages, and after a long moment said, "I wonder [if] he sneaks the cat in his house." Late in the story, Solomon Singer does sneak a cat into the hotel where he lives. My guess is that Cody wondered how the character accomplished this.

"Yeah, good question, Cody!" was an immediate response from one of the other children.

I took a moment to introduce the idea that in Open Forum, children can build off each other's comments. I instructed Cody to ask whether other readers had responses to his comment, and we saw the beginning of a true give-and-take between a couple of children.

"Would anyone like to respond to my question?" he asked.

Dylan responded. "He snuck the cat into his house so he wouldn't be lonely and I think he always wanted a cat in his apartment." Ultimately, of course, that give-and-take is the heart of Open Forum. We saw a glimpse of it on the first day!

By the end of this first Open Forum the children had become accustomed to saying, "Would you like to share?" and "Yes, thank you." They reminded each other not to raise their hands and not to begin speaking until everyone was listening. It was a first foray into the world of give-and-take in conversation, and these six-year-olds settled into that world as if they'd been doing it for years.

Open Forum is just one type of sharing, or reflecting, at the end of reader's workshop. In Erin's classroom, it would also have been effective to ask children to share with a partner what they learned about themselves as readers or to do some written reflection on how asking questions helps them as readers. A small group of children might have worked together to add to an anchor chart about questions or reconvened to share questions about a book they had all read. Ask your students—they'll have plenty of suggestions for ways to share their thinking.

Looking Back

This lesson was, in my experience, very typical of initial instruction on a strategy and a new type of sharing, but I was reminded how engaged children are when they have an opportunity to explore a wonderful book and how eager they are to discuss their observations and insights. I noticed how quickly very young children learned to use a cognitive tool—questioning—that is very abstract and how they used it to dig beneath the surface into the unwritten nuances in a text. They jumped right in to Open Forum and would have continued long past lunchtime, if that had been an option.

These were children who were more than eager to learn; they were ravenous. They quickly forgot the cameras and lost themselves in the book. They listened to their classmates and gravitated toward the implicit meanings in the book. Many couldn't wait to share their thinking. They were still thrusting up their hands to share in the waning moments of the lesson. They rushed back to apply what we had discussed in their independent reading and reconvened happily forty-five minutes later to share their thinking again in an Open Forum. They were just learning to read, but they certainly knew how to think and they couldn't get enough of it. I am convinced that their thirst for intellectual stimulation is not unique; all children harbor this longing to be challenged, to be engaged in great conversation. This could be any school in this country.

Looking back on that rainy day at Kolmar, when the children expected to see Helen Keller and got Ellin Keene, I'm taken aback by the subtleties of instruction and how much teachers multitask. I was exhausted after trying to integrate good strategy instruction, the Outcomes of Understanding, and the Talk About Understanding Principles, but I can't imagine any task more stimulating, more intellectually challenging. I was delighted with the first graders' stamina and engagement, but couldn't help thinking—how much further might we have gotten if I had only probed a bit more deeply with Canyon? What message would Kahlil have walked away with if I hadn't kept pushing him? What if Gina hadn't posed her initial question—the generative question—about whether the waiter was truly an angel? It all would have been different.

When you have a moment to reflect on your instruction, consider the staggering number of decisions you make and how much those decisions affect your students. Consider how lucky your students are to have a teacher who trusts the depth of their intellect and facilitates their conversations in a way that leads them to deeper understanding. Remind yourself that, though the instructional path you've chosen is not the easiest way to teach, it is the one that will have the most lasting value for children.

8

When We Respond to Children's Voices

With cameras rolling, a dozen teachers observing, and a teacher (me) who had never worked with his class before, John squirmed a bit and looked like he might be ready to share his synthesis with the class. You may recall the lesson, described and viewed in Chapter 5, in which I used the book *Hidden Witness* by Jackie Napolean Wilson in a fifth-grade classroom at Kolmar Elementary. The lesson focus was an introduction to synthesis and at the point I'm about to describe, I had already read a couple of the short photo essays, and the class was well into describing their syntheses. The children were talking about how their thinking about slavery changed when they came to realize that some slaves were actually brought into the homes of the masters, where they were treated a bit more fairly, and some had even been clothed well and taught to read.

The forthcoming interaction with John hit the cutting-room floor, but I still use it in work with teachers because John reinforced how our responses to children's oral language make a huge difference in their comprehension.

I called on John, an English language learner, though I could tell he was still looking unsure about sharing with the group. He asked, with respect to the slaves we were discussing in the book, "How do they know they're pregnant?"

I paused a moment, frantically trying to sort out where this out-of-the-blue question might have come from. I restated: "John, you're wondering how slave women knew when they were pregnant?" When in doubt, restate and fake it until you figure out where you're going! "Yeah, how did they know when they were pregnant?" I must have looked confused, so he repeated, "How did they know they were *pregnant*?"

I confess that my first instinct was to tell John that we could discuss his question later and move on to other children's responses! But by now, he was adamant. He had a question and he wanted an answer. He asked again, "How did they know they were pregnant?" The rest of the class was riveted, the observing teachers were looking at me with particular intensity, and I was asking myself how on earth I was going to get out of this one.

"John," I asked, "when you were thinking about how they knew when slave women were pregnant, what did you think about just before you had that question?" I know that kids don't tend to ask completely random questions; he was clearly intent on getting to the bottom of his query and I had to think there was something just underneath the question. Perhaps his question might have been better answered during "family life" week, but I also believed he had something to say about the essay.

He paused for a moment and then said, "At first I was thinking, how could they keep working when they were pregnant? Then I thought, did they treat them nicer when they were pregnant? Did they let them go?" I reminded myself—there is *always* something meaningful behind their responses, even if that meaning isn't immediately clear to us.

"You were wondering if slave owners treated slave women more fairly and humanely when they were pregnant." My hope was that by restating, I could get him to probe his thinking even more deeply.

"Yeah, but how would they know if they were pregnant?" THEY! The whole time he had been asking about how the *slave owners* knew when slaves were pregnant—how did *they* know?

"Okay, John, I understand that you wanted to know about the slave owners—you want to understand what happened to women working in the slave owners' homes when they were going to have children of their own."

"I want to know if you're a mom, do they be nicer to you?" He was trying to sort out how a slave owner would know when a slave was pregnant and was hoping against hope that such women would have been treated more equitably. He was, no doubt, considering the immense difficulty of working under the conditions we'd been discussing and trying to bear and raise children. Our talk about how some slaves were treated more humanely spurred hope in John. My initial assumptions about his question couldn't have been further off point, and it took several restatements and probing to uncover John's sensitive and insightful thinking.

This chapter is about how we respond to children's oral language contributions even when they are ambiguous to us—as John's response was, initially, to me. We'll explore the second set of five Talk About Understanding Principles, which relate to our responses to children and how they may deepen understanding. These are principles six through ten, shown again in Figure 8.1 (which is the same as Figure 6.1). All describe ways in which we can appropriately respond to children's spoken contributions in small groups, large groups, and/or conferences.

Responding to Children's Talk—Using the Second Five Talk About Understanding Principles

6. **Use silence** frequently, giving students an opportunity to think about concepts; serve as a model for taking time to think.

Typically, it's only with our most intimate companions that we appreciate silence in the presence of others. I love, for example, reading in the same

Talk About Understanding Principles:
Ten Ways to Modify Language to Enhance Understanding

Initiating Talk with Children (Chapter 6)

To enhance understanding when teaching or talking informally to students, we should:

1. **Vary the tone of our speech—speak in the quietest tone** appropriate for the situation. Garner children's attention by speaking more quietly, not more forcefully.

2. **Vary the pace** of our talk depending on the context and the content.

3. **Vary the intensity and expression of emotion** we use verbally and nonverbally to reveal which concepts and ideas are most essential for children to understand and remember.

4. **Use sophisticated vocabulary**, but define the words in the context of the discussion; use these words repeatedly.

5. **Speak with heightened civility and respect**, making clear the distinction between settings in which informal language is appropriate and serious learning situations that require more formal, academic language.

Responding to Children's Talk (Chapter 8)

To enhance understanding when we're responding to children's talk, we should:

6. **Use silence** frequently, giving students an opportunity to think about concepts; serve as a model for taking time to think.

7. **Restate and probe** children's responses during discussions, giving them a chance to reflect on what they have said and to probe ideas further.

8. **Label children's ideas with language you want all children to use;** display the language your community uses to describe thinking and use the same language consistently when describing comprehension strategies and the Outcomes of Understanding.

9. **Use varied syntax**—vary the length of sentences, depending on the purpose and content of instruction. Expand what children are saying into more fully developed sentences without changing the central ideas they are trying to communicate.

10. **Encourage children to engage in spirited and informed discourse about ideas**; show passion, surprise, and moments of insight about ideas. Model what it means to **consider the perspectives of others in conversation** and revise one's knowledge and beliefs because of those perspectives.

Figure 8.1

room, at the same time, with my family. We call it side-by-side reading. I love the opportunity to lose myself in thought about a book or in my writing with the people I love most nearby, doing the same thing. There is an intimacy and trust in the silence that I would like to evoke more frequently in schools.

In many situations, however, especially in today's classrooms where children are productive through conversation and where ideas are discussed frequently, most of us tend to fill the quiet spaces with our talk. If a child hesitates when responding to a question, we quickly move on to another child, saying, "That's okay, honey, if you think of what you wanted to say, raise your hand again. Anyone else?" Ironically perhaps, I have found that silence—not imposed, punitive silence, but the silence of thought—may be one of the most powerful oral language tools at our disposal. Silence buys us (and children) the time to think more deeply instead of saying the first thing that may pop into our heads. It's very interesting that children find it much easier than adults to be comfortable in silence, though we often assume otherwise. Children are often able to understand and express their insights in much greater depth when given the gift of silence. If we value deeper understanding, we're the ones who need to get more comfortable with silence.

I learned to use silence after watching myself on video. In old footage, I found myself teaching with a sense of urgency. I was trying to get way too much content squeezed into a small window of time without enough regard for how students were processing the information. In the guise of enthusiasm, I found myself talking almost as a way to figure out what I wanted to say rather than taking time to gather my thoughts and speak more concisely. Now, I'm working toward the judicious use of silence in my instruction.

In large and small groups, my goal is often to think aloud as I'm reading aloud so these lessons become key opportunities to incorporate silence. If I'm thinking aloud about asking questions while I read *An Angel for Solomon Singer* by Cynthia Rylant, for example, I might say something like the following:

"When I see the reflections of the Indiana countryside here in these illustrations of the streets and buildings of New York City, I wonder, does Solomon Singer use his memories of growing up in Indiana to ease his

> Children are often able to understand and express their insights in much greater depth when given the gift of silence. If we value deeper understanding, we're the ones who need to get more comfortable with silence.

loneliness? I wonder if it works, I wonder if the pain of living someplace where you're not happy is made just a bit easier by living in your memories. But I have another question, too. Wait. I need a moment to think about it. Could you give me some time in silence to think about this question, because it's not fully formed in my mind?"

At this point, several hands will go up, trying to "help" me find my thoughts, but it's important to model that *I don't need help, I just need time.* I will provide them with the same in return! I may say, "Thank you, but I just need a moment to think," and look down. I might resume twenty to thirty seconds later by saying, "Okay, my question is clearer to me now. Here's what I want to ask. I wonder if it's healthy to live in your memories, to let your memories of another time and place overwhelm the present— the life you're trying to lead right now. I wonder if Solomon Singer might find real happiness by finding something to love about the place where he *does* live rather than searching his memories for happier times. I'm still not sure whether I think living in your memories is a helpful or harmful thing. Maybe it can be both . . . "

I need to use silence in my think-alouds and other instruction in large and small groups, but I also need to encourage children to do the same. My hope—and there are times when we need to make this explicit—is that children will watch me using silence in the middle of a lesson and learn that it's okay, even preferable, to take time to think about something. Too often we encourage them to speak about the very first thing on their mind with the knowledge that, as soon as they utter it, the teacher will move on to another child with his hand up. This is not the way to deeper understanding.

Kaitlin was a second grader when I visited her classroom in suburban Chicago. She had watched me incorporate silence into my lesson at two different intervals and had turned to a partner to share inferences about the book *The Librarian of Basra.* "I infer," Kaitlin said in an almost inaudible voice, and then looked at her partner. "I just need time to say what I'm going to say." Kaitlin looked down for about ten seconds while her partner looked around. She finally looked up and her partner snapped right back into the conversation. Kaitlin said, "I infer that she [the librarian] is taking care of the books in the library because of the war—that's not the inference part! The inference is that she's taking care of the books in the library the same way we would take care of something, like our dog or our mom, because we love them so much." Don't you love the way the dog came before the mom! "The inference is that there are just some things that you want to take care of so much that you could even get caught in a war and you would still take care of it!"

My guess is that Kaitlin's inference was more thoughtfully considered in the moment she took to formulate her thinking. I heard several other children saying things like, "I infer that the librarian really likes those books." While that is certainly an inference, Kaitlin's went deeper—she probed the librarian's motivation to save books from a library in the heat of war. She empathized by putting herself in that position and noting that there are just some things and some people you take risks to protect.

If her partner had said, "What else, Kaitlin?" instead of, "Okay, now it's time for my inference!" it would have been even better! I was so interested to hear what Kaitlin might say next. It reminded me that I needed to focus on helping children ask follow-up questions when a partner has made a statement.

When the time to turn and talk was over, I pointed out to the children that Kaitlin had taken time in silence to think before she spoke and that her inference had been important because of that time. My hope was that other children would begin to value taking time to think.

I also encourage children to take their time when they want to share in front of the group. When a child raises her hand but offers a somewhat superficial comment, I follow up by saying, "What else? What else were you thinking?" If they say, "I don't know," I use my favorite line, "I know you don't know, but what would you say if you did know?" This is often met by silence, and it is into that void I am so tempted to leap. I have learned to become the queen of wait time. I sometimes have to bite my tongue—literally—to keep from leading the witness by saying, "Honey, is this what you were thinking . . . " Those silences while children are thinking about what to say next can feel the most uncomfortable to us. I encourage you to wait them out! If you must say something, say to the rest of the group, "I'm so impressed with the way Daniel is taking his time to think. I wish more kids did that. He knows we have plenty of time for him to take his time in silence to think." But then, wait. Wait. Wait. Wait. The time in silence is not harming them, it's helping! The time in silence is underscoring how important it is to continue to scan your mind for thoughts that might be relevant or insightful.

Some teachers find the use of silence particularly difficult in a conference. When you're one-on-one with a student, there seems to be some sort of unwritten expectation that someone has to be talking all the time. I encourage you to break through that expectation and actually teach children, right there in the conference, to use silence to their advantage. If you're focused, for example, on how a child did in working toward a particular goal set in the last conference, let the child search for evidence of progress without a running commentary from you. Work to get comfortable with the time you're spending with that child and avoid the temptation to look around the room, remind other children to focus, or make comments about how well everyone is doing. Just wait in silence. You're giving the child the message that nothing is more important to you in that moment than him and that you have all the time in the world (I know you don't) to wait while he thinks of what he'd like to say. I try to express appreciation and respect when he does respond.

Once a child has started to speak in a conference, focus on taking notes rather than giving immediate feedback. Let yourself have time to reflect on what the child is saying about her reading, withholding comment until she has had time to speak. Then consider asking, "What else?" Those two words may be the most powerful tool we have in comprehension instruction. Though kids may not be aware of it, there is *always* something else on their minds and more likely than not, their second and third comments about a book are likely to be more profound than the first.

7. **Restate and probe** children's responses during discussions, giving them a chance to reflect on what they have said and to explore ideas further.

It is no great revelation that teachers today feel enormous pressure to cover curriculum and rush through the scopes and sequences, pacing guides, and lesson plans districts often mandate. Children who struggle are pulled out during crucial periods of instruction, interruptions abound, and teachers are asked to keep track of an overwhelming amount of student

The time in silence is underscoring how important it is to continue to scan your mind for thoughts that might be relevant or insightful.

data, most of which is not descriptive enough to provide guidance for instruction. We're altogether too focused on testing outcomes that can never describe the complexity of children's learning, yet the decisions that are based on these can dramatically change the lives of children and their teachers. All of this can lead to a mind-numbing pace in the classroom and, as any reader of this book will know, that kind of pace is not conducive to in-depth thought and lasting understanding. The dilemma has become so acute, in fact, that some teachers have moved into other professions, others succumb to the breakneck pace by skimming over content, and the vast majority of us do the best we can in the context of policies that don't always support effective teaching and learning.

I want to suggest that, in our own way and in the precious time we have with students, we *can* find times to slow the pace and deepen the focus; and the collective influence of those moments of intellectual depth will have a much greater impact than we might imagine when we're caught up in the frenzy of it all. This slowing down requires us to exercise a certain discipline and relies on a steadfast belief in the capacity of *all* children to contribute brilliant insights to classroom discourse. It requires us to pause, wait, use silence, prompt, scaffold, restate, and probe, but it can be done, and it *is* being done in classrooms all over the country where teachers know that there are moments within each day when they can create the conditions most conducive to in-depth understanding.

Amanda Carey is an inspiring young fifth-grade teacher in Blue Springs, Missouri, whose interactions with children embody the aforementioned discipline and focus. As I observed in her classroom one morning, I was struck by a sense of calm; a feeling that she and the children had all the time in the world to explore a book and for them to read independently. They could dwell in the book and linger over their responses to it. There were periods of silence even as the whole class met, just to think through an idea. It was as if the hands on the clock weren't turning and nothing was more important than the ideas they were exploring that morning.

The Talk About Understanding Principles are alive and well in Amanda's classroom, though she isn't ticking off each principle in a robotic way—okay, I varied my tone and pace; okay, now I've shown different levels of emotion; great, now they've had some time in silence to think. All

I want to suggest that, in our own way and in the precious time we have with students, we *can* find times to slow the pace and deepen the focus; and the collective impact of those moments of intellectual depth will have a much greater impact than we might imagine when we're caught up in the frenzy of it all.

ten are seamlessly woven into her interactions with and reactions to children's comments in the classroom. One principle, however, stood out on the most recent day that I observed Amanda. She is extremely skilled in helping children explore their thinking more deeply following an initial response—she restates and probes.

When I entered the classroom on that chilly morning, the class was working in a crafting session using the book *Heroes* by Ken Mochikuzi. The children had just turned to talk to one another and were sharing their insights with the whole class. The first comment I heard Amanda make as I settled in and opened my computer was, "Desiree, how does your thinking relate to what Brad just shared?" Amanda avoided the fallback response of "Thanks, Desiree, that's good thinking; anybody else?" She restated what Desiree said to give everyone time to consider it more deeply and went the next step toward pulling others into the conversation. Amanda was showing the children how one comment is generative—it can and often does lead to fresh, new thinking about a book. She was helping them to see that their contributions don't exist in a vacuum—they can relate to others' ideas; being part of a group involves being influenced by others, considering their perspectives, perhaps even altering their own point of view because of the interaction. Amanda asked one simple question and opened up a world of possibility in terms of building on the conversation.

Rachel spoke on behalf of her partner next. She said, "Becca and I were talking about [what would happen if] second graders [were] reading this book and if they [would] have empathy for that character. We think they could because they've felt that emotion before. We were also talking about how it's [understanding the book] not just surface level, it's that you can go deeper when you talk about how you feel about it."

This presented what I think was an interesting moment for Amanda. The children had just shared a couple of insightful statements and it was difficult to know where to go next. One's instinct is to praise them and move on, but Amanda had another idea.

"So you think that, at least in a book like this, it helps you understand better if you talk not just about what is happening, but how you *feel* about the events and characters?" She restated the comment, but phrased it as a question, which led Rachel to say more.

"Yeah. We talked about how you could do that in almost any book. You can read it, but stop to think about your feelings and they're sort of like the characters'. But it doesn't happen in every book. Sometimes you don't feel the characters' [feelings]."

"Rachel and Becca," Amanda began, "you've raised something very important about the choices readers make. You're saying that, not in all books, but in some, perhaps those that are most important to you, you can stop or slow down your reading to purposefully think about the characters' feelings and sort of double-check inside of yourself to see if you're experiencing the same feelings. If you are, that would be a form of empathy. You would be feeling empathy. But I think it's important for us all to know that from the very beginning you said that you can *choose* to go beyond understanding the book at the surface level—those were your words. One way to go beyond the surface level is to pause and give yourself a chance to consider the characters' feelings. Did I get that right?" The girls nodded and Amanda continued.

"I'm wondering something else, though. You were talking about empathy for the characters' feelings, but you didn't yet say what those feelings were—I mean what you felt and what you think other readers, like second graders, might feel as a result of thinking about the characters' feelings."

In this interaction, Amanda restated, which gave the girls a chance to think about what they had said so far, but she probed further. It would have been so easy to thank them for their contributions and move on to another child, but she stuck with them, which makes it more likely that they'll think more deeply about the book and therefore retain and reapply the ideas they take from it. She wasn't disappointed.

Becca spoke this time. "I think it's how most people feel left out sometimes. The thing it makes me think about, though, is why do people do that to each other? Why do people, like back then in World War II, but also today, like why do people do stuff to make other people feel left out? Some people, grown-ups, kids, even if they're nice can make you feel so left out."

Becca not only showed empathy for the character, she also demonstrated thinking that extended beyond the book. She extrapolated from the book's message to the larger context of why people behave the way they do. If you refer back to the Outcomes of Understanding discussed in

Chapter 2, you'll see that Becca's comments exemplify outcome 8. She is building upon a detail from the text, considering her own emotions related to that detail, but also speculating on how that detail relates to a larger issue in the world—what leads people to mistreat fellow human beings. In many classrooms, the interaction might have stopped at "good job, girls, thanks for sharing," or "wow, that's great," but in Amanda's classroom, she restated and probed until she helped them reach deeper into their well of understanding.

There is little question that Amanda's way of responding to the girls took more time. She won't hear from as many children and some may have felt disappointed because they were unable to share that day. I propose, however, that her students benefited more from hearing in-depth thinking about the book than if four or five children had shared but had no chance to probe their ideas. The best thinking, as I often tell children, takes the longest time, but it's not only a function of time. We must facilitate their responses by restating them, in more complex and sophisticated language, and by asking them to pursue their thinking more deeply. The deeper thinking is *there* and we can help children access it and articulate it, first by believing that it's there and then by providing the time and scaffolding to allow them to plumb the depths. It's not difficult to restate and ask, "What else?" but it *is* challenging to convince ourselves to take the necessary time, given the urgency that characterizes contemporary classrooms. When we do, we will not be disappointed.

> *T*he deeper thinking is *there* and we can help children access it and articulate it, first by believing that it's there and then by providing the time and scaffolding to allow them to plumb the depths.

8. **Label children's ideas with language you want all children to use;** display the language your community uses to describe thinking and use the same language consistently when describing thinking strategies and the Outcomes of Understanding.

I will retell here a story my dear friend Colleen Buddy shared about a student named Nelson in her first/second-grade classroom in Lone Tree, Colorado. She was teaching inference as a comprehension strategy and was focusing one morning on predicting, a type of inference. She spoke about how predicting permitted readers to look into the future at events and outcomes that might happen, but nothing was certain. Readers have to hold their predictions in their minds and attend carefully to see if their prediction is confirmed. Nelson raised his hand after this description and asked a simple, but memorable question. "Mrs. Buddy," he began, lisping slightly due to the dearth of teeth in his mouth. "Mithus Buddy. How come when we're in reading you talk about predicting and when we're in science you talk about hypothesizing [hypothethizing] and when we're in math you talk about estimating [ethimating]. Aren't they really all the same thing?"

Nelson's question has long remained in my mind—he articulated something I had often neglected in the day-to-day flurry of school. We must name and describe thinking processes consistently and help make the connections among disciplines clear. Nelson was absolutely right, of course. Estimating, hypothesizing, and predicting (at least for a primary-grade child) depend on the same type of cognition—thinking into the future and then attending carefully to see if one's thinking is validated. I'm not suggesting that we should use only one of those terms—there are subtle, but important differences between them as we move further into the complexity of the discipline—but when we do introduce them, we must point out and engage children in conversation about how similar the thinking processes are.

There are dozens of similar examples. When we talk about drawing conclusions in science, we are talking about a type of inference. When we speak about the main idea in reading, we are really talking about a narrow form of determining importance, and when we talk about inquiry in science, we're describing asking questions, a process critical to deep understanding across the disciplines. I'm arguing that we need to first label those types of thinking, then make the connections among them explicit, and finally engage children in discussing how one type of thinking applies across the content areas.

Recently, I've been interested in the links between understanding art and understanding text. I love the visual arts and find that many of the cognitive tools I use when I look at a painting are applicable to understanding text. I began to look at the Outcomes of Understanding as lenses through which I might teach children to describe their thinking about paintings. I found that many of the Outcomes and Dimensions of Understanding I described in *To Understand* (Keene 2008) prove useful as cognitive (and behavioral) tools we can apply to help children understand their responses to paintings (see Appendix C, "Dimensions of Understanding," on the book's website). We can then ask them for insights about how their thinking about a painting can inform their thinking about reading. Take a moment to study the comparisons outlined in Figure 8.2 and consider the possibility of using art in your classroom to help children gain insight, not only into art, but into the ways in which they understand text.

Mackenzie is a fourth grader in Stephanie Dean's classroom at Cordill-Mason Elementary in Blue Springs, Missouri. On a recent afternoon, as a blizzard swirled outside and the children prepared for an early dismissal (not the kind of conditions that lead to in-depth thinking, by and large!), she stared at a painting called *Lighthouse Hill*, by Edward Hopper. I had read portions of a book entitled *Edward Hopper: Summer at the Seashore* (Lyons 2002), which introduces children to Hopper and his mid-twentieth-century paintings. Mackenzie paused as she absorbed the details in the painting and then said, "I love this picture. I want to be there—I could live in that old house and play on the porch and climb up to the top of the lighthouse." As she spoke, she never looked away from the painting. She continued, "I can imagine cars filled with people coming to see this place. It's so beautiful that tourists would come to see it and just stand there looking all around them. I think there are fields behind it where people are farming."

When she finished, I knew I had to carefully consider my response. I started by saying, "Mackenzie, that's amazing," and realized that was empty praise. I tried again. "The way you just described *Lighthouse Hill*, the way you talked about it, the strong emotions you have when you look at it. When you feel that way about something—when you find something very beautiful and you feel like, in this case, the painting was almost painted *just for you*, Mackenzie—that's called a *sense of the aesthetic*. You don't necessarily have the same feeling about all paintings or even all of Edward Hopper's paintings, but for some reason that is almost hard to describe, you feel that this painting is uniquely beautiful and that you want to remember it for a long, long time."

My goal was to label her thinking in a way that not only she, but also her classmates would be able to use later to describe similar experiences. Her teacher, Stephanie, wrote the word *aesthetic* on chart paper and I continued

How We Understand Art and Text	
Understanding Art	**Understanding Text**
When we study art, we are **engaged with the piece**, focused on particular details; we are lost in the world created by the painting or sculpture.	When we read, we are deeply **engaged**—we experience a sense that the world around has disappeared and we are subsumed by the world of the text.
When we study art, we notice different details and dimensions each time we view a painting or sculpture; **the piece may appear changed** when revisited or discussed with another viewer.	When we read, we can define and describe **how our thinking has changed** in the course of reading or rereading.
When we study art, we may experience a **memorable emotional response**—the sense that what we feel as we view the piece may be part of our emotional life for a long time.	When we read, we **experience a memorable emotional response**—the sense that our reactions to the text may be part of our emotional life for a long time.
When we study art, we **experience the aesthetic**. Particular works may be compelling to us in a way we find difficult to describe—we find a distinct beauty, a sense that piece has a personal meaning or message for us.	When we read, we **experience the aesthetic**—we feel a desire to linger with or reread portions of the text we find beautiful, well-written, surprising, or moving. We want to experience portions of the book again and we may wish that the book wouldn't end.
When we study art, we may **dwell for long periods of time** with a particular piece. We may discover details we missed originally. We may "enter into" the painting to **imagine what is not shown**.	When we read, we **ponder**—we feel a desire to **pause and consider** new facets and twists in the text. We may want to reread in order to think more about certain ideas.
When we study art, we may **use particular "filters"** to view a piece—we may look at details such as the source of the light, the motion implied, or the emotion suggested by the piece.	When we read, we **recognize patterns and symbols**. We may experience a moment of insight or begin to use our knowledge of literary tools to recognize themes and motifs as well as symbols and metaphors in stories.
When we study art, we may draw conclusions about the **artist's intent, values, emotional state, or perspective**; we may be aware of how the artist **affirms or challenges our beliefs, values, and opinions**.	When we read, we are aware of the **author's intentions, values, and claims**; we are attuned to the ways he/she **affirms or challenges our beliefs, values, and opinions**.
When we study art, we may **experience insight**. We may come to understand our own emotions or experiences in a new way, possibly due to our efforts to see patterns and symbols in the piece.	When we read, we **experience insight**—we experience and can describe a moment of clarity, of "seeing" for the first time, possibly due to our efforts to recognize patterns and structures in text.
When we study art, we may **remember**—the piece becomes a familiar and well-loved memory we can clearly recreate in our minds.	When we read and understand, we **remember**—we reapply previously learned concepts and ideas in new learning situations.

Figure 8.2

to speak about what it means to react to the particular beauty of something like a painting. I tried to use the word *aesthetic* numerous times so that Mackenzie and the other children would begin to connect the sound of the word to its meaning and to the word on the chart paper.

I was curious about the connection Mackenzie might make to her reading, though. I asked a follow-up question. "Mackenzie, I'm wondering now if you think that responding to a painting aesthetically tells you anything about your reading. Do you think that you've ever experienced a sense of the aesthetic during reading?"

She responded immediately and enthusiastically (and for a prolonged period of time!) described a scene from the Harry Potter book she was reading. She described it in great detail, and just when I thought that all we were going to get was a blow-by-blow retelling of a scene, Mackenzie added, "It's just the same as when you're looking at a painting. You have to read it over and over to feel that way—I felt like my heart was pounding and I couldn't wait to find out what happened, but I wanted to hear the words again in my head. It's just like how we took a long time to look at that painting. You have to keep looking and looking at something or you don't see it all."

What she was describing, of course, was how to understand anything— a book or a work of art; we have to give it some time, look at the detail in the painting, reread a section of the book, in order to be overwhelmed by a sense of the aesthetic. Several of her classmates also made clear connections between their experiences in looking at Hopper paintings and what they do, cognitively, as they read. Mackenzie was also showing signs of dwelling for a long period of time with a painting (and a book!) and entering into the painting to imagine what is not shown (these are markers of understanding listed in Figure 8.2).

It made me wonder why we don't use paintings and the other arts, to which children respond so viscerally and so spontaneously, to help them gain insight into how their mind works when trying to comprehend concepts across the content areas and the texts they read. Do we feel like we don't have time? I wonder, had we not had that conversation in Stephanie's classroom that day, if the children (a) would have had a chance to spend a long time looking into the heart of a painting, viewing beyond the boundaries of the canvas to the emotional heart of the painting, and (b) would have made the

It made me wonder why we don't use paintings and the other arts, to which children respond so viscerally and so spontaneously, to help them gain insight into how their mind works when trying to comprehend concepts across the content areas and the texts they read.

connections between the thinking processes we use to understand a painting (or a concept in social studies, for that matter) and the ways we approach understanding a text.

We had an opportunity to talk about how those who seek to understand *dwell* in the concept, text, or painting until details and emotions are revealed that they otherwise might have missed. To label what they have experienced—in this case responding to Mackenzie's aesthetic reaction by labeling it for the class—is to solidify the fleeting moment and make it possible that they will have similar reactions in very different contexts going forward.

We teachers have some experience in labeling thinking. The strategies many of us teach (see Appendix B, "Comprehension Strategies Defined," on the book's website)—to help students comprehend more deeply and lastingly, for example—are labels for thinking processes the profession has agreed upon over the years. Sharing those labels with children enables them to become more independent in using the strategies and to describe their thinking in a way others will understand. Children can choose to question, infer, use images, or determine importance, for example, when they understand the thinking process that label represents. In thousands of classrooms, teachers have found that explicit instruction in comprehension strategies empowers students to understand more completely and enables them to define and describe their thinking to others (Keene and Zimmermann 2007).

Comprehension strategies are often explicitly taught—we initiate instruction on them—but we must also consider how we *react and respond* when children share their thinking spontaneously. We need to begin to listen "between the lines," even when their descriptions are rudimentary. Teachers have become skilled, for example, in labeling a "text-to-text connection" when a child links ideas from two or more books. There are many other important ideas that children share, however, that need to be labeled and defined in order to be useful in the future. Think about the Outcomes of Understanding described in Chapters 2 and 4, for example. These labels offer ways to respond when children are working to understand deeply, but don't have the language to articulate their thinking.

I conferred not long ago with Samantha, who was reading Laura Ingalls Wilder's classic *Little House in the Big Woods*. Samantha looked at me and described the plot with some urgency. There was a blizzard raging and the family was running out of food, she told me, but she knew it would be "okay because Laura is the kind of character that is strong when other kids wouldn't be. She figures out how to solve stuff." I responded by telling Samantha that she was describing *advocacy* (Figure 2.1, outcome 6). When a reader feels that she is "behind" the character, rooting for him or her, predicting a particular outcome and hoping for that outcome, she is advocating for the character. I took a moment to write the word in several forms—advocacy, advocate, advocated—in her reader's response journal and shared examples of the sense of advocacy I've felt in books and in the world. If, in future reading, Samantha feels that she is "getting behind" a character, I hope she'll use the term *advocacy*. When she does, other readers in her classroom will have a chance to build their repertoire of labels that describe deeper understanding.

9. **Use varied syntax**—vary the length of sentences, depending on the purpose and content of instruction. Expand what children are saying into more fully developed sentences without changing the central ideas they are trying to communicate.

"It's an epidemic," said one teacher in the audience of a workshop I was leading. Teachers were sharing their frustration about students who, when they do share their thinking, do so in very rudimentary ways—incomplete sentences, pronouns with unclear references, colloquialisms that we, sitting here in another generation, may not understand.

"It's because they spend their lives in front of screens—video games, computers, smartphones, movies. They don't have anyone to interact with. You don't learn to speak well when you're interacting with a screen," another teacher interjected.

It's hard to argue with their conclusions. I, too, find it very frustrating when students communicate in truncated sentences. I think about very young children who have yet to develop the oral language that permits them to fully express their thinking. I worry that the language structures they use are prohibiting them from fully sharing their thoughts and I'm concerned that we may come to the erroneous conclusion that their thinking isn't very complex or sophisticated.

I believe that the vast majority of children are thinking about far more complex and abstract ideas than their spoken language enables them to

I believe that the vast majority of children are thinking about far more complex and abstract ideas than their spoken language enables them to communicate. I want them to be able to make their thinking public, and there is often a tremendous mismatch between the depth of their ideas and what they actually say.

communicate. I want them to be able to make their thinking public, and there is often a tremendous mismatch between the depth of their ideas and what they actually say. However, we can either spend our time bemoaning the "screen generation" or we can figure out what to do about it. It may be true that many of today's students haven't benefited from "table talk" or "car conversations" with parents and friends as we would hope, but it's time to acknowledge that we are the ones who are going to help them speak in a way that actually reflects the depth of their thinking. I try to keep four things in mind when responding to a child whose syntax is not fully developed:

1. Listen intently for a line of thinking that may indicate the meaning they are trying to communicate.

2. Restate the child's thinking in a more syntactically complex way and check to see whether your interpretation is correct.

3. Don't change the child's intended content, insert your ideas, or "lead the witness" to say what *you're* thinking.

4. Ask the child to restate his/her thinking using more sophisticated syntax.

During the filming of the video footage for this project, we captured a conference I had with twelve-year-old Marco that perfectly exemplifies this dilemma and almost drove me into another line of work.

"Dunno." Marco shrugged his shoulders and uttered the inimitable "dunno" that every teacher has heard tens of thousands of times. Sitting next to his desk for our conference, but surrounded by observing teachers and cameras, I engaged in a quick mental battle. I was inclined to let Marco off the hook. It was nearly time to bring the class back together for reflecting and he clearly didn't want to share his thinking with me. The observers and cameras were overwhelming, I reasoned. On the other hand, if I accepted Marco's "dunno" I might inadvertently communicate to him that I didn't *expect* him to have or share any thinking.

The class was studying determining importance and I had read a portion of *Delivering Justice: W. W. Law and the Fight for Civil Rights* by Jim Haskins. The whole class had had a good discussion about W. W. Law's contributions to the civil rights movement, and everyone was reading books related to the movement in their independent reading time. It would have been easier to tell Marco that we'd confer another time, but I just couldn't bring myself to do that.

"Marco, in the crafting session today, we talked about how someone who spent his life as a mailman found the time, strength, and capacity of character to lead others. I'm curious. Did you find anything we read or discussed important enough to remember?" He looked annoyed. He now knew that I wasn't going to let "dunno" stand.

"Not really," he said. "He was a leader."

"He was a leader," I repeated, somewhat awkwardly.

Silence. The teachers stopped taking notes.

I waited with the book on my lap. Not comfortable. Finally, I opened the book and began to thumb through the pages. "As you look back over the sections we read today, Marco, I wonder if you think anything here is important."

"Not really."

I again considered other careers I might have chosen. I was inclined to selling furniture at Crate and Barrel at that moment. Think how much fun it would be to help people with scads of money furnish their big homes! The second hand on the classroom clock stopped. I swear it stopped.

"Okay, Marco. I'm going to share something that I felt was very important in this book and then you can let me know if you think anything is important. Does that sound like a plan?" No response. My thinking was that I had probably not done enough thinking aloud for Marco. I have to watch myself to avoid the situation where I read aloud, pause to think aloud a couple times, and expect the students to automatically start using the strategy. They need more scaffolding: They need more thinking aloud, they need to see all the factors a proficient reader considers when deciding what's important. I turned to a page that describes the Savannah Boycott—some African Americans' 1960 decision to boycott stores that had mistreated them terribly.

"Marco, when I read this page, I think about how brilliant this boycotting strategy was. W. W. Law and others had tried every other way to get white business owners to treat them fairly, and finally they cut them off economically. They cut off their business in these stores which, of course, hurt the store owners financially. I think that it's very important to think about how they chose a variety of ways to make their point, and that the one that worked was actually the economic strategy. The white business owners began to respond when African Americans stopped shopping with them. I think that's important because I think it says something about those business owners. They wouldn't respond when African Americans appealed to their sense of what was right—they responded when the money stopped flowing from a whole lot of customers."

Marco was definitely following what I said. He looked back at the page and said, "That was a long time ago." I admit I had no idea where he was going, or what to say in response.

"Well, it was happening when I was a very little girl, so a long time ago, but not so very long ago, if you think about the history of this country."

"That wouldn't happen today," Marco said, looking at the book.

"You think that this wouldn't happen today?"

"Yeah. No. No one would do that—what he did."

This interaction is, in my experience, very common. Marco was speaking in very aborted, simple sentences, filled with pronouns with uncertain antecedents. I just wasn't following him. The sentence structure of his short utterances was itself confusing.

"So, let me see if I understand you, Marco. It is your belief that there aren't people around today who would . . . " I paused because I really wasn't sure what he was trying to say.

"Who would get them together like that," Marco replied. It was becoming clearer. I had found what I believed to be the line of thinking he was trying to express. I began to think less of my discomfort than of what must be terribly frustrating for Marco. Can we even imagine how exasperating it must be to have an idea and be unable to fully communicate it?

"You're wondering if there are people like W. W. Law around today who organize people to protest policies that are unfair?"

"Uh-huh."

"Marco, I'd like for you to tell me again because what you're saying is very important. I want to be sure I understand exactly what you mean, so take a second and repeat your idea for me. Use some of the words I used, combine them with your words, and say the whole idea again."

"Well, today it wouldn't happen that way. There aren't some people who would get everybody together to not buy stuff like that."

We were now well into the reflecting time, and the second hand on the clock had not only started again, it was threatening the end of the class period.

"You're saying that today . . . " I didn't get to finish the restatement.

"Today there are things that are unfair too. Still, blacks don't get treated right. Who is there to make them get together to say that it's wrong?"

I restated what he had said and encouraged him again. "Marco, start from the beginning. Tell me again."

He was exasperated, but by now it was very important to him to get his idea out. The observing teachers leaned forward.

"I'm trying to say that today we don't have people like they did then. I mean, who are they? No Martin Luther King, no W. W. Law. Who . . . "

I interrupted, "Do you mean who *organizes*?"

"Yeah! Who organizes people to get them together to show white people what is still unfair? Who talks to kids who say bad stuff about kids who are different?"

Whew! From "that wouldn't happen today" to "who organizes people" is a long stretch, but Marco had an important point to make and was inhibited by his oral language. I struggled for a long time before I could put my finger on what he was trying to say, but when I did, we were able to move forward.

Two things stand out as I reflect on that conference. First, Marco needed me to think aloud *in the conference* before he was clear on his own ideas about the book. I try to remember to carry the book I've used in the crafting session with me when I confer for just that reason. Second, it was critical to press on after I finally understood his point. If I had stopped the conference once I figured out what he was trying to say without asking him (which is not an altogether easy thing to do) to repeat and expand his thinking in more and more complex sentences, he would have missed the opportunity to learn how to more skillfully articulate his very important ideas. Asking him to restate his idea several times led him to be clearer and more expansive in his description.

When very young children are first learning to speak, caretakers naturally use what is known as expansion of telegraphic speech. When a year-old child asks his father for more milk, he may say, "Mo mil." His father's immediate response is to say, "Oh, Jacob, you want more milk. You must be so thirsty! You're drinking a lot of milk today." This expansion picks up on the thread of meaning the child expressed and places it into several fully formed sentences, thereby modeling words and syntactic structures the child will eventually use to get his needs met. We need to do something very similar when working with children in school. We must expand their telegraphic speech and give them the syntactic structure they need to unearth their thoughts.

The conference with Marco took longer than I had planned. We ran right up to the end of the period and there was no reflecting opportunity for the rest of the students that day. It's a trade-off and, in that circumstance, I'm glad I tipped the scale toward Marco. I believe that he discovered a trove of ideas below the surface and began to trust that he had the capacity to share them with others. Is that time well spent? I believe so. These are the weighty judgment calls we make each day.

10. **Encourage children to engage in spirited and informed discourse about ideas**; show passion, surprise, and moments of insight about ideas. Model what it means to **consider the perspectives of others in conversation** and revise one's knowledge and beliefs because of those perspectives.

I love a good argument. I have a wonderful group of women friends who gather nearly every weekend to linger over dinner, debate political issues, react to world events, talk about what we've been reading, and think together about workplace problems (one of my best friends is an employment attorney who always has great stories to share). We send each other articles and respond to each other with reactions and, occasionally, disagreements. When we're joined by my husband (who cancels me out in the voting booth) or others who challenge our ideas, it gets even better. I love the moment when I feel that I've made a strong argument (rarely!) or when someone hops on to the point I am making. I even like to acquiesce when someone makes a stronger argument.

When I was growing up, both of my grandfathers were state senators in Colorado—on opposite sides of the aisle. I love my memories of their spirited debates over holiday dinners and remember how they "competed"

We must expand their telegraphic speech and give them the syntactic structure they need to unearth their thoughts.

to recruit my brother and me into their own political party. In the end, they were the best of friends and their discourse was very civil; one would often concede a point to the other, but they had very different ways of viewing the world. I love politics, relish debates, and actually look forward to big election years. I know what you're thinking, and it probably does indicate that I need serious therapy! (I also love to fly, so that should confirm any lingering doubts you had about my overall stability.) But there is rich learning embedded in debate. I have found that, to make a strong argument, I have to understand the topic well. I have to have read about it, discussed it, heard others' opinions, and worked to understand their perspective before I can clearly articulate my point of view.

All of this leads me to wonder about the role of debate and argument in classrooms today. Do we raise issues that lead to argument, in the most positive sense of the word? Do we model ways to build and defend an argument? Do we help children recognize and empathize with others' perspectives? Are the books we read, the topics we discuss, worthy of debate? In my experience, children are at their most engaged when they are in the heat of debate. We can't create those conditions every day, of course, but when responding to the ideas students share, I think it makes sense to consider encouraging healthy debate every once in a while.

Creating an opportunity for this type of discussion doesn't have to be formal or planned—a debate can arise spontaneously, if we're listening carefully to what children share with us. I recently taught a demonstration lesson on determining importance in a fifth-grade class using the book *My Secret Camera: Life in the Lodz Ghetto* by Frank Dabba Smith. *My Secret Camera* uses photographs taken from inside the Lodz ghetto in Poland during the Second World War to tell the story of a prisoner, Mendel Grossman. Grossman was determined to document the unbearable conditions there and, though he died on a forced march and many of his negatives were destroyed, a few photos survive. Smith narrates the book in first person as if he were Grossman, who hid his camera and took photographs when he hoped none of the Nazi guards were watching.

I read the first few pages, including a section in which Grossman climbs to the top of a building to photograph fellow prisoners below. He indicates that his own heart is weak and that his friends tell him he should

Do we raise issues that lead to argument, in the most positive sense of the word? Do we model ways to build and defend an argument? Do we help children recognize and empathize with others' perspectives? Are the books we read, the topics we discuss, worthy of debate?

not be documenting life in the ghetto this way—it is too dangerous. I stopped there to think aloud. "I think it's important so far to be aware of the risk he is taking to get these shots. If Mendel is caught, it's hard to imagine what the consequences would be."

Tara raised her hand. "If he didn't do it, though, how would we ever know about how bad it was in there? Was he the only one with a camera? What if no one ever told about the way life was in there?"

Garrett immediately straightened up and said, "It's good that he took those pictures so we know now what it was like there." Others nodded in agreement, and this was a decision point for me. It would have been natural to resume reading at this point, but I wanted to see if I could help them adopt a slightly different perspective and engage in an informal debate about these issues. I actually adopted a different position than the one I took before the children spoke.

"I see your point, Tara and Garrett, and I want you to think about something else. Grossman worked alongside other men, women, and children in Lodz. Some of the photos we've seen show him in groups, even taking pictures of his friends." I wasn't sure if they had enough schema to realize that the Nazis might well punish a whole group for the "transgression" of one among them. I just let the comment sink in for a moment.

"Oh!" Ali nearly jumped up from the floor. "He could really get those other people in trouble. If they were near him when he got caught, the Nazis could do something to all of them, even the kids."

"Okay, Ali, you're saying that he might implicate his friends and other prisoners if he is caught. They stand the chance of being punished for something they didn't do if Mendel is caught." I wanted to restate with slightly more elevated syntax and vocabulary and provoke additional discussion. "Is it right then, for Mendel to take the photographs at all? He's documenting the conditions inside the camp, but he's putting his friends at risk as well as himself."

"He had to," Thomas added. "The rest of the world had to know what was going on in there and at the beginning of the book it said that the ghettos were secret. People on the outside didn't know they were in there."

"I don't think it was fair," Ali jumped back in. "If his friends got caught too, they would be treated badly, even starved, when they hadn't done anything."

I interrupted the discussion to read a bit further into the book, telling them to "think about how you feel about this question. Did Mendel have a responsibility to the rest of the world to get photos of the ghetto out and to document what they were enduring inside, or was it wrong of him to endanger others around him for the sake of his photos?"

I paused again after showing them a photograph of a group of children hauling a heavy plow-like device down a street. They were straining against the load and the few words on the page describe Mendel Grossman's hope that the world would see how the young boys had to suffer. "I think it's important to notice how young these boys are," I said. "These children are younger than you and their labor is immensely difficult."

"I've been thinking about whether he should take these pictures or not," Roberto interjected. "And I think he should. Maybe that's [the presence of the pictures] why we don't have kids working too hard today."

"Okay, Roberto, so you think, because some of these pictures survived and the world knows of the Nazis' crimes against children, that humanity has learned from this and that we no longer condone child slavery and child labor?"

"Yes." Roberto paused for a moment, then added, "And maybe it made it easier even for us. Maybe kids today are treated better because people saw the pictures and said it's wrong."

Samuel jumped in. "Yeah, but it still doesn't explain why he thought it was okay to get other people caught. Those boys could have been killed just because he was taking their pictures, even though they were working the way they were supposed to."

At that point, I paused to ask the children to turn and talk to the person sitting closest to them. I wanted everyone to have a chance to share his or her perspective on the growing debate. When they came back together, the argument continued with even greater fervor. It was all I could do to facilitate the discussion with so many children wanting to jump in.

Later, though this was not initially a planned part of the lesson, I asked the children to write about their argument, even if they had a more nuanced view and could understand both sides. In reviewing the written arguments later, I have to admit that the group discussion had far more passion than the ideas that made it to the paper. I reflected about how I might have structured that activity differently to help them bring the spark of the oral discussion into their writing, but concluded that there are just times when the conditions are right and the book conducive to a great discussion in the group. Herein lies the discomfort for many of us. Was it worth the time it took? What about the kids who didn't participate in the whole-class discussion? How do we know if they "got it"? How do you assign a grade to something like this?

I believe that we need to be more comfortable with these ambiguities. Though it is difficult to fully document the discussion (we did that day because cameras were rolling!) and impossible to assign a "grade" to students' thinking, I left certain that they gained additional perspective on the horrors faced by Jews in that era and even came to understand themselves better because they took a position in the debate. The children who didn't jump into the group discussion were still witnessing a spirited debate, one to which the class can return and invite their ideas. We may not be able to say that their contributions that day constituted an "A" or a "B," but when it comes to real understanding—the kind that lasts—the debate, the emotion it sparked, the fact that we were discussing real events, the shock of some of the photographs, and the reality of one man's dilemma in the chaos of WWII will, I believe, remain in their hearts and minds.

We may not be able to say that their contributions that day constituted an "A" or a "B," but when it comes to real understanding—the kind that lasts—the debate, the emotion it sparked, the fact that we were discussing real events will, I believe, remain in their hearts and minds.

*****

The Talk About Understanding Principles I've discussed here and in Chapter 6 are only guidelines. You already incorporate many of them into your daily teaching and there are, undoubtedly, other oral language practices that would enhance understanding in the way that these have for me. I introduced them to spark perhaps a new level of consciousness about the impact of our discourse with children on the depth of their understanding. I do, however, acknowledge that it is very difficult to observe oneself while teaching; it's tough to catch ourselves using some of the ineffective oral language habits described in Chapter 6 and it's not always obvious to us when we are using the Talk About Understanding Principles.

For these reasons, I've created a simple tool you and your colleagues can use to observe each other with an eye toward becoming more aware of the discourse in your classroom (see Appendix F, "Oral Language

Reflection Tool," on the book's website). I hope this tool will bring you and a colleague into each other's classrooms to focus on this critically important component of daily teaching.

It probably goes without saying that I hope you have read this book alongside others, perhaps in a study group, and that there are a couple of brave souls among you who are willing to launch this self-study. After all, I've let you look in on my teaching, good, bad, and ugly, in this book! Isn't it time to invite a colleague to help you do the same?

POSTLUDE

Every Child, Every Time

We all have moments from our teaching lives that are indelibly etched in memory. I will never forget the fifth and sixth graders who welcomed me back to the classroom with signs and hugs and cards following the week I was gone when my mother died. I was twenty-one. Some of them were twelve. Not much difference in our ages when you think about it, but they knew how to bring me back into their world, which I sorely needed.

I have a note in my office from Ben, then a fifth grader in Blue Springs School, Missouri. It reads, "I love the way you make people think harder and harder. I didn't know I could think that deep[.] I loved trying to find information that I didn't know I had in my brain. Thank you." I taped it to my bookshelf to remind myself why I keep standing in TSA lines, getting on airplanes, and waking up in hotels forgetting where I am. It's more than enough.

As much as I treasure those moments, none has ever brought me to tears. Until May 2011. I was completing a Heinemann Residency (in which I work with a school or district for multiple days over the course of a year or more) in Delaware, Ohio. Barbara Keister, a superb literacy coach, and her colleague Amy Carroll, a great third-grade teacher, asked me to confer with Alex one afternoon.

Alex, I was told, was new to Amy's classroom, had attended many previous schools, and was having a difficult time focusing. He wandered around the room, had relatively little stamina for reading, cried frequently, and, if he suspected that he wasn't succeeding, he simply gave up rather than continuing the task.

When I sat down to confer with Alex, a dozen teachers observing, I quickly saw why Amy and Barb were concerned about him. I asked him to share his thinking about his book. He demurred. I asked him to share his thinking about the book Amy had read aloud to the class. He demurred. I asked him to share questions he had about either book. He demurred. He began to look around the room, squirmed, and demurred some more. He looked at me as if to say, "Don't you get it? I don't really have anything to say. I'm considering a move to pull the fire alarm which, I hope, will lead this group of teachers and especially *you* out of this room. Maybe they'll forget me in the process." I can also imagine what the observing teachers were thinking. "We spent how much money to bring this person into the district . . . " I started to squirm. *I* considered getting up to pull the fire alarm. They waited. Alex looked around the room.

As I waited, I reminded myself that, too often, I ask a child to show evidence of thinking or engage in some other task that I haven't adequately modeled. I wondered if that was the case with Alex. When teaching comprehension, we're asking children to do some very complex thinking. They need multiple exposures to our think-alouds before they can reasonably be expected to manipulate their thinking in the same way. I told Alex that I had a number of questions from the read-aloud text and asked if he would be interested in hearing a couple of mine. Then it would be his turn to share. He listened. He asked a question that related only minimally to the book. I asked another. He tried again.

The conference evolved into a "my turn, your turn" volley of questions in which Alex was wholly engaged. I taught him about generative questions—one question that leads to another and another—and he delved in more deeply. Each question was more thoughtful and relevant than those that preceded it; each time he asked a question, he became more focused. His expression was intense, he leaned forward.

Later, as Amy gathered the class into a circle for reflection, I happened to sit on the floor behind Alex. Several children shared what they had learned about themselves as readers or questions they had about the books they were reading. Alex volunteered and told the class about generative questions. He made an intellectual contribution to the group.

A few minutes later, he turned to me, looked at me directly, and said simply, "I feel smart."

There it was. The moment that keeps me getting on airplanes and staying in hotels. My eyes brimmed over and I couldn't quite get my composure back. The child sitting next to Alex noticed the sniffling, turned around, and immediately notified the rest of the room. "Something's wrong with her!" he blurted. Actually, nothing was wrong at all.

I believe it's important to scrutinize those breakthrough moments for the lessons they offer. It's true that the conference took longer than it was "supposed" to. It's true that Alex was uncomfortable (as was I) for a time. It was quiet and awkward for a few minutes. I was reminded, however, that when we talk about every child learning at high levels, when we post banners and mission statements proclaiming that we believe in helping children become lifelong learners, when we are emphatic about never giving up on children who struggle, we mean *every child, every time.* Intellectually, we all know this is true, but we're so often worried about the time—how long is this conference, what if I don't get to confer with all the children this week, is that pair in the corner focused on their work, what if we're late to Music, what if I don't cover the necessary skills before the assessments? *Every child, every time.*

I hope Alex learned that Amy, Barb, his other teachers and I will never, ever give up. We will wait him out, model some more, and *know* that he will share relevant, insightful, even profound thinking about books and the ways they connect to the world. I hope he remembers that this level of thinking is within him and accessible. I hope he recalls how great it felt to feel smart.

Alex's words were simple and barely audible. "I feel smart." My mother used to say, "In simplicity is found the greatest elegance." Alex helped me understand what she meant. It is often the most simply stated, barely-audible words that resonate most deeply. Sometimes, those words echo for years before we fully understand. Do we give adequate thought to them? Do we sculpt them in a way that facilitates deeper understanding? Have we adequately focused on the markers of deeper understanding in our classrooms? As always, I close this book with more questions than answers. I like it that way. It reassures me that years from now, I'll still seek to understand the most compelling ways we can help children gain insight into the world and feel smart.

Many of the words we choose and certainly the way we express them will become imprinted in our children's minds and hearts. We have control over them. We can choose the way we convey ideas, the way we encourage children to share their thinking. Much of the artistry in teaching is woven into those oral interactions with children, and there will always be a place for that artistry. When we seek to understand what it means to understand and when we share those insights with children, don't we all feel smart? In the end, that's the all-important foundation of our work with children. We leave them with the intellectual curiosity and sense of efficacy to continue the exploration into understanding the world, long after we've faded from their memories.

References

Bautista, Elvia. 2006. "Remembering All the Boys" from *This I Believe*. New York: Holt.

Beck, I., M. McKeown, and L. Kucan. 2002. *Bringing Words to Life*. New York: Guilford.

Bomer, K. 2010. *Hidden Gems: Naming and Teaching from the Brilliance in Every Student's Writing*. Portsmouth, NH: Heinemann.

Duke, N. K. 2000. "3.6 Minutes Per Day: The Scarcity of Informational Texts in First Grade." *Reading Research Quarterly* 35: 202–224.

Durkin, D. 1979. "What Classroom Observations Reveal About Reading Comprehension Instruction." *Reading Research Quarterly* 14 (4): 481–533.

Fisher, D., and N. Frey. 2009. *Background Knowledge: The Missing Piece of the Comprehension Puzzle*. Portsmouth, NH: Heinemann.

Johnston, P. 2004. *Choice Words*. Portland, ME: Stenhouse.

Keene, E. O. 2006. *Assessing Comprehension Thinking Strategies*. Long Beach, CA: Shell.

———. 2008. *To Understand: New Horizons in Reading Comprehension*. Portsmouth, NH: Heinemann.

Keene, E. O., et al. 2011. *Comprehension Going Forward*. Portsmouth, NH: Heinemann.

Keene, E. O., and S. Zimmermann. 2007. *Mosaic of Thought: The Power of Comprehension Strategy Instruction*. Portsmouth, NH: Heinemann.

Kempton, S. 2007. *The Literate Kindergarten*. Portsmouth, NH: Heinemann.

Miller, D. 2002. *Reading with Meaning*. Portland, ME: Stenhouse.

———. 2008. *Teaching with Intention* Portland, ME: Stenhouse.

Neret, G. 2000. *Michelangelo, 1475–1564*. Koln, Germany: Taschen.

Nichols, M. 2008. *Talking About Text: Guiding Students to Increase Comprehension Through Purposeful Talk*. Huntington Beach, CA: Shell.

Pearson, P. David, and M. C. Gallagher. 1983. "The Instruction of Reading Comprehension." *Contemporary Educational Psychology* 8: 317–344.

Pressley, M. September 2001. "Comprehension Instruction: What Makes Sense Now, What Might Make Sense Soon." *Reading Online* 5 (2). Retrieved 6/10/11 from http://www.readingonline.org/articles/handbook/pressley.

Tovani, C. 2000. *Do I Really Have to Teach Reading?* Portland, ME: Stenhouse.

———. 2004. *I Read It, But I Don't Get It*. Portland, ME: Stenhouse.

CHILDREN'S BOOKS

Bunting, Eve. 1999. *Smokey Night*. New York: Sandpiper Houghton Mifflin Books.

———. 2006. *One Green Apple*. New York: Clarion Books.

———. 1995. *Cheyenne Again*. New York: Clarion Books.

Cisneros, Sandra. 1984. *The House on Mango Street*. New York: Alfred Knopf.

Coles, Robert. 1995. *The Story of Ruby Bridges*. New York: Scholastic.

Creech, Sharon. *A Fine, Fine School*. New York: HarperCollins.

Drew, David. 2000. *Amazing Animals*. New York: Houghton Mifflin Harcourt.

Fox, Mem. 1985. *Wilfrid Gordon McDonald Partridge*. La Jolla, CA: Kane/Miller Publishers.

Haskins, Jim. 2005. *Delivering Justice: W. W. Law and the Fight for Civil Rights*. Cambridge, MA: Candlewick Press.

Johnston, Tony. 2004. *The Harmonica*. Watertown, MA: Charlesbridge Publishing.

Le Tord, Bijou. 1999. *A Bird or Two: A Story About Henri Matisse.* Grand Rapids, MI: Eerdmans Books for Young People.

Lyons, Deborah. 2002. *Edward Hopper: Summer at the Seashore.* New York: Prestel Verlag.

MacLachlan, Patricia, and Emily MacLachlan. 2003. *Painting the Wind.* New York: HarperCollins.

Mochikuzi, Ken. 1997. *Heroes.* New York: Lee & Low Books.

Morrison, Toni 2004. *Remember: The Journey to School Integration.* New York: Houghton Mifflin.

Polacco, Patricia. 1998 *Thank You, Mr. Falker.* New York: Philomel Press.

Rylant, Cynthia. 1996. *An Angel for Solomon Singer.* New York: Scholastic.

Smith, Frank D. 2000. *My Secret Camera: Life in the Lodz Ghetto.* New York: Harcourt.

Stott, Carole. 2009. *Space Exploration.* New York: DK Children's Books.

Weatherford, Carole B. 2005. *Freedom on the Menu: The Greensboro Sit-Ins.* New York: Dial Books.

Wilder, Laura Ingalls. 1953. *Little House in the Big Woods.* New York: HarperCollins.

Wilson, Jackie Napolean. 1999. *Hidden Witness: African-American Images from the Dawn of Photography to the Civil War.* New York: St. Martin's Press.

Woodson, Jacqueline. 2007. *Our Gracie Aunt.* New York: Hyperion.

Credits *(continued from page iv)*

Consider the Heinemann Residency

Access long-term, customized literacy-action planning delivered directly by Ellin Oliver Keene.

The **Keene Residency** provides powerful professional development designed to improve engagement and literacy learning for children in grades K–8. Ellin helps schools assess and identify their strengths and their professional development needs. Through carefully crafted on-site PD, Ellin will engage your colleagues in a manner that helps schools sustain and extend the momentum for positive change following the residency.

Each Keene Residency from Heinemann includes:

- **Pre-assessment of the school's needs** and assistance in development of a literacy action plan

- **Customized and collaborative planning** between Ellin and the Leadership Team prior to the residency

- **Four or five days of intensive on-site professional development** divided into two visits to deliver initial PD and responsive follow up support

- **Rigorous, in-depth professional learning experiences** offered in a variety of formats

- **A comprehensive follow-up plan** created by Ellin to help you sustain and enhance the momentum

- **A library of Heinemann professional books** and materials to support further professional study.

heinemann.com/pd

from **Ellin Oliver Keene**

*The more a teacher understands about the nature of reading itself, the more he or she will be able to develop a palette of instructional strategies to respond to and challenge each student appropriately.* 99

—*Ellin Oliver Keene*

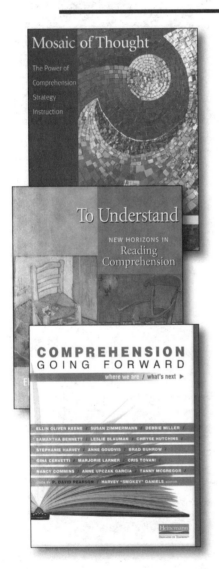